Augustus C. Thompson

Lyra Coelestis

Hymns on heaven

Augustus C. Thompson

Lyra Coelestis
Hymns on heaven

ISBN/EAN: 9783337083014

Printed in Europe, USA, Canada, Australia, Japan

Cover: Foto ©Thomas Meinert / pixelio.de

More available books at **www.hansebooks.com**

Lyra Coelestis.

In some hour of solemn jubilee
The massy gates of Paradise are thrown
Wide open, and forth come in fragments wild,
Sweet echoes of unearthly melodies,
And odors snatched from beds of amaranth,
And they that from the crystal river of life
Sprung up on freshened wing, ambrosial gales!
The favored good man in his lonely walk
Perceives them, and his silent spirit drinks
Strange bliss, which he shall recognize in heaven.

COLERIDGE.

Lyra Cœlestis.

HYMNS ON HEAVEN.

SELECTED BY

A. C. THOMPSON, D. D.,

AUTHOR OF "THE BETTER LAND," "MORNING HOURS AT PATMOS," "GATHERED LILIES," ETC.

BOSTON:
GOULD AND LINCOLN,
59 WASHINGTON STREET.
NEW YORK: SHELDON AND COMPANY.
CINCINNATI: GEORGE S. BLANCHARD.
1863.

PREFACE.

MANY of the pieces in this volume are not easily accessible to the majority of readers. No intentional alterations have been made, except omissions and change of titles. Besides the hymns originally English, there will be found translations from the Syriac, Latin, Russian, German, French, Italian, Spanish, and Portuguese. The volume, however, does not profess to be a complete anthology in this department of religious literature. Sufficient materials for a second series remain even now in the hands of the compiler.

A. C. T.

CONTENTS.

Where is Heaven?

What is Heaven?

I. THE BETTER COUNTRY.

II. THE HOLY CITY.

III. THE PLACE OF REUNION.

CONTENTS.

IV. OUR REST.

Who are in Heaven?

I. OUR GOD.

II. OUR SAVIOUR.

CONTENTS.

III. HOLY ANGELS.

IV. SAINTS GLORIFIED.

V. OUR SAINTED FRIENDS.

VI. REDEEMED CHILDREN.

What are they Doing in Heaven?

What is the Way to Heaven?

What is it to go to Heaven?

CONTENTS.

Who would not go to Heaven?

I. ASPIRATIONS AFTER HEAVEN.

II. LONGING TO BE WITH JESUS.

How soon in Heaven?

How Long in Heaven?

I. TILL THE RESURRECTION.

II. FOR EVER AND EVER.

Index of First Lines.

INDEX OF FIRST LINES.

Hymns on Heaven.

WHERE IS HEAVEN?

Beyond the River.

DUBLIN UNIV. MAGAZINE.

TIME is a river deep and wide;
And while along its banks we stray,
We see our loved ones o'er its tide
Sail from our sight away, away.
Where are they sped — they who return
No more to glad our longing eyes?
They've passed from life's contracted bourn,
To land unseen, unknown, that lies
Beyond the river.

'Tis hid from view, but we may guess
How beautiful that realm must be;

For gleamings of its loveliness,
  In visions granted, oft we see.
The very clouds that o'er it throw
  Their veil, unraised for mortal sight,
With gold and purple tintings glow,
  Reflected from the glorious light
    Beyond the river.

And gentle airs, so sweet, so calm,
  Steal sometimes from that viewless sphere;
The mourner feels their breath of balm,
  And soothed sorrow dries the tear;
And sometimes listening ear may gain
  Entrancing sound that hither floats —
The echo of the distant strain
  Of harps and voices, blending notes,
    Beyond the river.

There are our loved ones in their rest!
  They've crossed Time's river; now no more
They heed the bubbles on its breast,
  Nor feel the storms that sweep its shore.
But there pure love can live, can last; —
  They look for us their home to share;
When we, in turn, away have passed,
  What joyful greetings wait us there,
    Beyond the river.

Up Above.

DUBLIN UNIVERSITY MAGAZINE.

Down below, the wild November whistling
  Through the beech's dome of burning red,
And the Autumn sprinkling penitential
  Dust and ashes on the chestnut's head.

Down below, a pall of airy purple,
  Darkly hanging from the mountain-side,
And the sunset from his eyebrow staring
  O'er the long roll of the leaden tide.

Up above, the tree with leaf unfading
  By the everlasting river's brink,
And the sea of glass beyond whose margin
  Never yet the sun was known to sink.

Down below, the white wings of the sea-bird
  Dashed across the furrows, dark with mould,
Flitting, like the memories of our childhood,
  Through the trees, now waxen pale and old.

Down below, imaginations quivering
  Through our human spirits like the wind,
Thoughts that toss, like leaves about the woodland,
  Hope, like sea-birds, flashed across the mind.

Up above, the host no man can number,
In white robes, a palm in every hand,
Each some work sublime forever working
In the spacious tracts of that great land.

Up above, the thoughts that know not anguish,
Tender care, sweet love for us below,
Noble pity, free from anxious terror,
Larger love, without a touch of woe.

Down below, a sad, mysterious music,
Wailing through the woods and on the shore,
Burdened with a grand majestic secret
That keeps sweeping from us evermore.

Up above, a music that entwineth
With eternal threads of golden sound
The great poem of this strange existence,
All whose wondrous meaning hath been found.

Down below, the church, to whose poor window
Glory by the autumnal trees is lent,
And a knot of worshippers in mourning,
Missing some one at the sacrament.

Up above, the burst of Hallelujah,
And (without the sacramental mist
Wrapped around us like a sunlit halo),
The great vision of the face of Christ.

Down below, cold sunlight on the tombstones,
  And the green wet turf with faded flowers,
Winter-roses, once like young hopes burning,
  Now beneath the ivy dripped with showers.

And the new-made grave within the churchyard,
  And the white cap on that young face pale,
And the watcher, ever as it dusketh,
  Racking to and fro with that long wail.

Up above, a crowned and happy spirit
  Like an infant in the eternal years,
Who shall grow in love and light forever,
  Ordered in his place among his peers.

Oh the sobbing of the winds of autumn!
  Oh the sunset streak of stormy gold!
Oh the poor heart, thinking in the churchyard
  Night is coming, and the grave is cold!

Oh the pale, and plashed, and sodden roses!
  Oh the desolate heart, that grave above!
Oh the white cap, shaking as it darkens
  Round that shrine of memory and love!

Oh the rest forever and the rapture!
  Oh the hand that wipes the tears away!
Oh the golden homes beyond the sunset,
  And the hope that watches o'er the clay!

Above the Skies.

PHILIP DODDRIDGE.

YE golden lamps of heaven, farewell,
With all your feeble light;
Farewell, thou ever-changing moon,
Pale empress of the night.

And thou, refulgent orb of day,
In brighter flames arrayed!
My soul, that springs beyond thy sphere,
No more demands thine aid.

Ye stars are but the shining dust
Of my divine abode,
The pavement of those heavenly courts,
Where I shall reign with God.

The Father of eternal light
Shall there his beams display;
Nor shall one moment's darkness mix
With that unvaried day.

No more the drops of piercing grief
Shall swell into mine eyes,
Nor the meridian sun decline
Amidst those brighter skies.

There all the millions of his saints
  Shall in one song unite,
And each the bliss of all shall view
  With infinite delight.

Heaven of Heavens.

EDMUND SPENSER.

Look thou no further, but affixe thine eye
  On that bright shynie round still moving masse,
The house of blessed God, which men call Skye,
  All sowed with glistring stars more thicke than grasse,
  Whereof each other doth in brightnesse passe,
But those two most which, ruling night and day,
As king and queene, the heavens' empire sway.

And tell me then, what hast thou ever seene
  That to their beautie may compared bee?
Or can the sight that is most sharpe and keene
  Endure their captain's flaming head to see?
  How much lesse those much higher in degree,
And so much fairer, and much more than these,
As these are fairer than the land and seas?

For farre above those heavens which here we see
  Be others farre exceeding these in light;
Not bounded, not corrupt, as these same bee,
  But infinite in largenesse and in hight,
  Unmoving, uncorrupt, and spotlesse bright,
That need no sunne t'illuminate their spheres,
But their own native light farre passing theirs.

And as these heavens still by degrees arize,
  Until they come to their first Mover's bound,
That in his mightie compasse doth comprize,
  And carrie all the rest with him around;
  So those likewise doe by degrees redound,
And rise more faire, till they at last arrive
To the most faire, whereto they all do strive.

Faire is the heaven where happy soules have place
  In full enjoyment of felicitie,
Whence they doe still behold the glorious face
  Of the Divine Eternall Maiestie;
  More faire is that where those Idees on hie
Enraunged be, which Plato so admyred,
And pure Intelligences from God inspyred.

Sometimes Seen.

BEYOND these chilling winds and gloomy skies,
  Beyond death's gloomy portal,
There is a land where beauty never dies,
  And love becomes immortal;

A land whose light is never dimmed by shade,
  Whose fields are ever vernal,
Where nothing beautiful can ever fade,
  But blooms for aye, eternal.

We may not know how sweet the balmy air,
  How bright and fair its flowers;
We may not hear the songs that echo there,
  Through those enchanted bowers.

The city's shining towers we may not see
  With our dim, earthly vision,
For death, the silent warder, keeps the key
  That opes those gates elysian.

But sometimes, when adown the western sky
  The fiery sunset lingers,
Its golden gates swing inward noiselessly,
  Unlocked by unseen fingers.

And while they stand a moment half ajar,
  Gleams from the inner glory
Stream brightly through the azure vault afar,
  And half reveal the story.

O land unknown! O land of love divine!
  Father allwise, eternal,
Guide, guide these wandering, way-worn feet of mine
  Into those pastures vernal.

Not Very Far.

H. BONAR.

SURELY, yon heaven, where angels see God's face,
  Is not so distant as we deem
From this low earth. 'Tis but a little space,
  The narrow crossing of a slender stream;
'Tis but a veil which winds might blow aside.
Yes; these are all that us of earth divide
From the bright dwelling of the glorified,—
  The Land of which I dream.

These peaks are nearer heaven than earth below,
  These hills are higher than they seem;
'Tis not the clouds they touch, nor the soft brow
  Of the o'er-bending azure as we deem.

'Tis the blue floor of heaven that they up-bear,
And, like some old and wildly rugged stair,
They lift us to the land where all is fair,—
 The Land of which I dream.

These ocean waves, in their unmeasured sweep,
 Are brighter, bluer, than they seem;
True image here of the celestial deep,
 Fed from the fulness of the unfailing stream,
Heaven's glassy sea of everlasting rest,
With not a breath to stir its silent breast,
The sea that laves the land where all are blest,
 The Land of which I dream.

And these keen stars, the bridal gems of night,
 Are purer, lovelier, than they seem;
Filled from the inner fountain of deep light,
 They pour down heaven's own beam;
Clear speaking from their throne of glorious blue,
In accents ever ancient, ever new,
Of the glad home above, beyond our view,
 The Land of which I dream.

This life of ours, these lingering years of earth,
 Are briefer, swifter, than they seem;
A little while, and the great second birth
 Of time shall come,—the prophet's ancient theme.

Then He, the King, the Judge, at length shall come,
And for this desert, where we sadly roam,
Shall give the kingdom for our endless home,
The Land of which I dream!

Everywhere Near.

H. BONAR.

Not from Jerusalem alone
To heaven the path ascends;
As near, as sure, as straight the way
That leads to the celestial day,
From farthest realms extends,—
Frigid or torrid zone.

What matters how or whence we start?
One is the crown to all;
One is the hard but glorious race,
Whatever be our starting-place.
Rings round the earth the call
That says, Arise, depart!

From the balm-breathing, sun-loved isles
Of the bright Southern Sea,
From the dead North's cloud-shadowed pole,
We gather to one gladsome goal, —
One common home in thee,
City of sun and smiles!

The cold rough billow hinders none,
Nor helps the calm, fair main;
The brown rock of Norwegian gloom,
The verdure of Tahitian bloom,
The sands of Mizraim's plain
Or peaks of Lebanon.

As from the green lands of the vine,
So from the snow-wastes pale,
We find the ever open road
To the dear city of our God, —
From Russian steppe, or Burman vale,
Or terraced Palestine.

Not from swift Jordan's sacred stream
Alone we mount above;
Indus or Danube, Thames or Rhone, —
Rivers unsainted and unknown, —
From each the home of love
Beckons with heavenly gleam.

Not from gray Olivet alone
  We see the gates of light;
    From Morven's heath, or Jungfrau's snow,
    We welcome the descending glow
  Of pearl and chrysolite,
And the unsetting sun.

Not from Jerusalem alone
  The church ascends to God;
    Strangers of every tongue and clime,
    Pilgrims of every land and time,
  Throng the well-trodden road
That leads up to the throne.

II.

What is Heaven?

WHAT IS HEAVEN?

I. THE BETTER COUNTRY.

The Goodly Land.

MRS. ANNE STEELE.

FAR from these narrow scenes of night
 Unbounded glories rise,
And realms of infinite delight,
 Unknown to mortal eyes.

Fair distant land! could mortal eyes
 But half its joys explore,
How would our spirits long to rise,
And dwell on earth no more.

There pain and sickness never come,
 And grief no more complains;
Health triumphs in immortal bloom,
 And endless pleasure reigns.

From discord free, and war's alarms,
And want, and pining care,
Plenty and peace unite their charms,
And smile unchanging there.

There rich varieties of joy
Continual feast the mind;
Pleasures which fill, but never cloy,
Immortal and refined.

No factious strife, no envy there,
The sons of peace molest;
But harmony and love sincere
Fill every happy breast.

No clouds those blissful regions know,
Forever bright and fair;
For sin, the source of mortal woe,
Can never enter there.

There no alternate night is known,
Nor sun's faint, sickly ray;
But glory from the sacred throne
Spreads everlasting day.

The glorious Monarch there displays
His beams of wondrous grace;
His happy subjects sing his praise,
And bow before his face.

Oh may the heavenly prospect fire
  Our hearts with ardent love,
Till wings of faith and strong desire
  Bear every thought above.

Prepare us, Lord, by grace divine,
  For thy bright courts on high;
Then bid our spirits rise and join
  The chorus of the sky.

The Land of Promise.

THOMAS OLIVERS.

THE God of Abraham praise,
  Who reigns enthroned above,
Ancient of everlasting days,
  And God of love;
Jehovah, great I AM!
  By heaven and earth confest,
I bow, and bless the sacred name,
  Forever blest.

The God of Abraham praise,
  At whose supreme command
From earth I rise, and seek the joys
  At his right hand;

I all on earth forsake,
  Its wisdom, fame, and power,
And him my only portion make,
  My shield and tower.

The God of Abraham praise,
  Whose all-sufficient grace
Shall guide me through this pilgrimage
  In all his ways;
He calls a worm his friend,
  He calls himself my God;
And he shall save me to the end,
  Through Jesus' blood.

He by himself hath sworn,
  I on his oath depend;
I shall, on eagles' wings up-borne,
  To heaven ascend;
I shall behold his face,
  I shall his power adore,
And sing the wonders of his grace
  For evermore.

Though nature's strength decay,
  And earth and hell withstand,
To Canaan's bound I urge my way
  At his command;

The watery deep I pass,
  With Jesus in my view,
And through the howling wilderness
  My way pursue.

The goodly land I see,
  With peace and plenty blest,
A land of sacred liberty
  And endless rest.
There milk and honey flow,
  And oil and wine abound,
And trees of life forever grow,
  With mercy crowned.

There dwells the Lord our King,
  The Lord our righteousness;
Triumphant o'er the world and sin,
  The Prince of peace
On Zion's sacred height
  His kingdom still maintains,
And glorious, with his saints in light,
  Forever reigns.

He keeps his own secure,
  He guards them by his side;
Arrays in garments white and pure
  His spotless bride;

With streams of sacred bliss,
  With groves of living joys,
With all the fruits of Paradise,
  He still supplies.

Before the Three in One
  They all exulting stand,
And tell the wonders he hath done
  Through all their land;
The listening spheres attend,
  And swell the growing fame,
And sing, in songs which never end,
  The wondrous name.

The God who reigns on high
  The great archangels sing,
And "Holy, holy, holy," cry,
  "Almighty King!"
Who was, and is the same,
  And evermore shall be;
Jehovah, Father, great I AM,
  We worship thee.

Before the Saviour's face
  The ransomed nations bow,
O'erwhelmed at his almighty grace,
  Forever new;

He shows his prints of love,
They kindle to a flame,
And sound, through all the world above,
The slaughtered Lamb.

The whole triumphant host
Give thanks to God on high;
Hail, Father, Son, and Holy Ghost,
They ever cry;
Hail, Abraham's God and mine,
I join the heavenly lays;
All might and majesty be thine,
And endless praise.

"No Night shall be in Heaven."

THOMAS RAFFLES.

No night shall be in heaven, — no gathering gloom
Shall o'er that glorious landscape ever come:
No tears shall fall in sadness o'er those flowers
That breathe their fragrance through celestial bowers.

No night shall be in heaven, — no dreadful hour
Of mental darkness or the tempter's power;
Across those skies no envious cloud shall roll,
To dim the sunlight of the enraptured soul.

No night shall be in heaven. Forbid to sleep,
These eyes no more their mournful vigils keep;
Their fountains dried, their tears all wiped away,
They gaze undazzled on eternal day.

No night shall be in heaven, no sorrow's reign,
No secret anguish, no corporeal pain,
No shivering limbs, no burning fever there,
No soul's eclipse, no winter of despair.

No night shall be in heaven, but endless noon;
No fast-declining sun, nor waning moon;
But there the Lamb shall yield perpetual light,
'Mid pastures green and waters ever bright.

No night shall be in heaven, no darkened room,
No bed of death, nor silence of the tomb;
But breezes ever fresh with love and truth
Shall brace the frame with an immortal youth.

No night shall be in heaven. But night is here —
The night of sorrow and the night of fear;
I mourn the ills that now my steps attend,
And shrink from others that may yet impend.

No night shall be in heaven. Oh had I faith
To rest in what the faithful Witness saith,
That faith should make these hideous phantoms flee,
And leave no night henceforth on earth to me!

No Graves are There.*

R. A. RHEES.

"No graves are there;"
No willow weeps above the grassy bed
Where sleeps the young, the fondly loved, the fair,
The early dead.

No funeral knell
Blends with the breeze of spring its mournful tone,
Bidding thenceforth those balmy breezes tell
Of loved ones gone.

O'er the cold brow
No bitter tears of agony are shed;
None o'er the still, pale form in anguish bow,
Whence life has fled.

"No graves are there;"
Nor sunny slope, green turf, or quiet grot,
Those sad mementos of departure bear,
For death is not.

That fearful foe,
Here ever bearing from us those we love,
Resistless as his power is owned below,
Has none above.

* Upon a tombstone in a churchyard at Bridgeton is a beautiful device. Over the memorial a hand is pointing to the skies; and forming an arch just above it is the triumphant exclamation—'There are no graves there.'—*Chris. Chron.*

No! in the tomb
Ends his dominion; there his power is o'er;
And they who safely tread its path of gloom
Shall die no more.

"No graves are there;"
Father, we thank thee that there is a clime
Guarded alike from death, and grief, and care,
Untouched by time.

We praise thy name,
That from the dust and darkness of the tomb
We can look up in faith, and humbly claim
Our future home.

Hasten the day
When, passing death's dark vale without a fear,
We, as we reach that heavenly home, may say,
No graves are here.

Where is no more Sea.

FYSH.

When tempests toss, and billows roll,
And lightnings rend from pole to pole,
Sweet is the thought to me,

That one day it shall not be so;
In the bright world to which I go
The tempest shall forget to blow;
  There shall be no more sea.

My little bark has suffered much
From adverse storms; nor is she such
  As once she seemed to be;
But I shall shortly be at home,
No more a mariner to roam;
When once I to the port am come,
  There will be no more sea.

Then let the waves run mountains high,
Confound the deep, perplex the sky,—
  This shall not always be;
One day the sun will brightly shine
With life, and light, and heat divine;
And when that glorious land is mine,
  There will be no more sea.

My Pilot tells me not to fear,
But trust entirely to his care,
  And he will guarantee,
If only I depend on him,
To land me safe, in his good time,
In yonder purer, happier clime,
  Where shall be no more sea.

Where the Blind See.

JESSIE GLENN.

OH, I hear them tell of a canopy fair,
That stretches its blue wing far up in the air;
They say it is gemmed with the stars of night,
That sparkle and gleam in the pale moonlight;
But when I look up all is darkness to me,
For I cannot see! I cannot see!

I hear of the flowers that round me bloom,
And my spirit finds joy in their sweet perfume;
The rose and the clematis surely are fair,
For feeling can tell me that beauty is there;
But those lovely tints are not painted for me,
For I cannot see! I cannot see!

The zephyr's sweet wing rustles over me now,
For I feel its soft breath fan the curls on my brow;
Hark! it speaks to me too, in its own sweet way;
Oh, would I might feel it, ere passing away!
I will touch it just once — but where can it be?
Oh, I cannot see! I cannot see!

The rays of the sun, which they tell me are bright,
I feel on my cheek, though a stranger to sight;
While music's low tones gently steal on my ear,
And while pining to see it I scarcely can hear;

But music and sunbeams are nothing to me,
For I cannot see! I cannot see!

The look of affection, how grateful to some!
And, caught from its beams, what fond feelings must
come!
Oh, would that its form could but dawn on my mind!
But a glance from a loved one is not for the blind;
Oh, why must this world be all darkness to me?
Why may I not see? why not see?

Then is there no joy for the sightless one? say,
Must the beauties of earth all unseen pass away?
Then I will look up to a bright world above,
Where all shall be happy and peaceful in love,
And there from this darkness my eyes shall be free,
For then I shall see! I shall see!

Where the Deaf Hear.

J. MONTGOMERY.

To me, though neither voice nor sound
From earth or air may come,
Deaf to the world that brawls around,
The world to me is dumb.

Yet may the quick and conscious eye
  Assist the slow, dull ear;
Light can the signs of thought supply,
  And with a look I hear.

The song of birds, the water's fall,
  Sweet tones and grating jars,
Hail, tempest, wind, and thunder, all
  Are silent as the stars —

The stars that on their tranquil way,
  In language without speech,
The glory of the Lord display,
  And to all nations preach.

Now, though one outward sense be sealed,
  The kind remaining four,
To teach me needful knowledge, yield
  Their earnest aid the more.

Yet hath my heart an inward ear,
  Through which its powers rejoice;
Speak, Lord, and let me love to hear
  Thy Spirit's still, small voice.

So when the Archangel from the ground
  Shall summon great and small,
The ear now deaf shall hear that sound,
  And answer to the call.

Oh, Paradise must Fairer be.

FROM THE GERMAN OF F. RÜCKERT.

Oh, Paradise must fairer be
  Than any spot below!
My spirit pines for liberty;
  Now let me thither go.

In Paradise, forever clear,
  The stream of love is flowing;
For every tear that I've shed here
  A pearl therein is glowing.

In Paradise alone is rest;
  Joy-breathing, woe-dispelling,
A heavenly wind fans every breast
  Within that happy dwelling.

For every wounding thorn below
  A rose shall blossom there,
And sweeter flowers than earth can show
  Shall twine around my hair.

And every joy that, budding, died,
  Shall open there in bloom;
And Spring, in all her flowery pride,
  Shall waken from the tomb.

And all the joys shall meet me there
  For which my heart is pining,
Like golden fruit in gardens fair,
  And flowers forever shining.

My youth that fled so soon away,
  And left me sad, decaying,
Shall there be with me every day,
  With bright wings round me playing.

All hopes, all wishes, all the love
  I longed for, tasted never,
Shall bloom around me there above,
  And be with me forever.

More Blest than Eden.

A. C. COXE.

There is a land like Eden fair,
  But more than Eden blest;
The wicked cease from troubling there,
  The weary are at rest.

There is a land of calmest shore,
  Where ceaseless summers smile,
And winds, like angel whispers, pour
  Across the shining isle.

There is a land of purest mirth,
  Where healing waters glide;
And there the wearied child of earth
  Untroubled may abide.

There is a land where sorrow's sons
  Like ocean's wrecks are tossed;
But there revive those weeping ones,
  And life's dull sea is crossed.

There is a land where small and great
  Before the Lord appear;
The spoils of fortune and of fate,
  Whom heaven alone can cheer.

There is a land where, star-like, shine
  The pearls of Christ's renown;
And gems, long buried in the mine,
  Are jewels in his crown.

There is a land like Eden fair,
  But more than Eden blest;
Oh for a wing to waft me there,
  To fly, and be at rest!

My Native Land.

FROM THE SPANISH OF ALDANA, BY LONGFELLOW.

CLEAR fount of light! my native land on high,
Bright with a glory that shall never fade!
Mansion of truth! without a veil or shade,
Thy holy quiet meets the spirit's eye.
There dwells the soul in its ethereal essence,
Gasping no longer for life's feeble breath;
But sentinelled in heaven, its glorious presence
With pitying eye beholds, yet fears not death.
Beloved country! banished from thy shore,
A stranger in this prison-house of clay,
The exiled spirit weeps and sighs for thee!
Heavenward the bright perfections I adore
Direct, and the sure promise cheers the way,
That whither love aspires, there shall my dwelling be.

"My Ain Countree."

N. Y. OBSERVER.

I AM far frae my hame, an' I'm weary oftenwhiles
For the langed-for hame-bringing, an' my Father's wel-
come smiles;
I'll ne'er be fu' content until my een do see
The gowden gates o' Heaven, an' my ain countree.

The earth is flecked wi' flowers, mony-tinted, fresh, an'
gay,
The birdies warble blithely, for my Father made them
sae;
But these sights an' these soun's will as naething be to
me
When I hear the angels singing in my ain countree.

I've His gude word of promise, that some gladsome day
the King
To His ain royal palace his banished hame will bring;
Wi' een an' wi' hearts running owre we shall see
The King in his beauty an' our ain countree.

My sins hae been mony, an' my sorrows hae been sair,
But there they'll never vex me, nor be remembered mair;
His bluid hath made me white, his hand shall dry
mine ee,
When he brings me hame at last to my ain countree.

Like a bairn to its mither, a wee birdie to its nest,
I wad fain be ganging noo unto my Saviour's breast;
For he gathers in his bosom witless, worthless lambs like
me,
An' carries them himsel' to his ain countree.

He's faithfu' that hath promised; he'll surely come again;
He'll keep his tryst wi' me, at what hour I dinna ken,
But He bids me still to watch, an' ready aye to be
To gang at ony moment to my ain countree.

So I'm watching aye an' singing o' my hame as I wait
For the soun'ing o' his footfa' this side the gowden gate.
God gie His grace to ilk ane wha listens noo to me,
That we a' may gang in gladness to our ain countree.

II. THE HOLY CITY.

The City of Peace.

FROM THE GERMAN OF A. KNAPP.

HOW the pilgrim, sad and weary,
Finds here a desert wild and dreary,
With shades of death and darkness filled;
Soon, with groves of palm surrounded,
The peaceful city shall be founded,
Which for his glory Christ shall build.
In splendid colors dressed,
On sapphires it shall rest;
Doors and windows
Of crystal rare, and turrets fair
Of richest gems, shall glitter there.

There, amid this palace royal,
A countless host, well tried and loyal,
Shall see the glory of their Lord;
All their fears and sorrows ended,
Shall they, with peace and joy attended,
Receive from him their rich reward.

The crown of righteousness
Shall there his people bless;
No destroyer
Shall thither steal to work their ill,
But Christ will there his grace fulfil.

When 'twill be — seek not to know it;
Who guides in his own time will show it,
And his own time is always best.
Heralds he abroad is sending,
That they, to all his grace commending,
May bring them all to seek his rest.
Enough for us to know
What he would have us do
Till the harvest;
The world's wide field its fruits must yield, —
The ransom was for all revealed.

Tell it now with joyful praises, —
"The Prince of Life his palace raises!"
O'er land and sea the tidings sound;
Not in vain his invitation;
The messengers of his salvation
Proclaim it to the poor around.
Beneath the burning sky
They to their work apply,
Daily sowing.

His word he'll keep; though now they weep,
With joy shall they the harvest reap.

Seeing growth they are requited;
With tears of joy, with souls delighted,
First-fruits they now are bringing on;
Where the ground to drought was given,
Head, hands, and hearts, they lift to heaven,
Admiring what the Lord has done.
All fresh with morning dew,
Green fields spring up to view,
Breathing fragrance;
For bitter sighs glad songs arise,
While hope anticipates the prize.

But the Lord, by varied trial,
Oft proves his heralds' self-denial,
And makes them wait, and toil, and mourn;
Oft will let fierce storms o'ertake them,
To hunger, thirst, and want forsake them,
To gloom their fairest prospects turn.
In his own chosen way
His wisdom he'll display,
Clearly teaching,
While deepest night brings on the light,
That what he does is always right.

Knowing this, shall fears beguile us?
Though traitors, leagued with foes, revile us,
Our onward course let us pursue;
They that, shame for Jesus bearing,
Will persevere, his way preparing,
Shall safely reach his glory too,
There, with the Son of God,
To join in blest abode
All the pious,
And freely own, through grace alone,
Their works of love and faith were done.

Ever shall thy praise be glorious,
When, over all their ills victorious,
Thy saints unite in tuneful strife.
They, from death by thee delivered,
Shall from thy love no more be severed;
Such is thy will, thou Prince of Life!
The world, Lord, rests on thee,—
Thy world with pity see!
Showing mercy
To him whose days are prayer and praise,
To him who yet in error strays.

The Holy Jerusalem.

FROM THE LATIN, BY WILLIAMS.

THE holy Jerusalem,
  From highest heaven descending,
And crowned with a diadem
  Of angel bands attending,
The living city, built on high,
Bright with "Celestial Jewelry!"

She comes, the bride, from heaven-gate,
  In nuptial new adorning,
To meet the Immaculate,
  Like coming of the morning;
Her streets of purest gold are made,
Her walls of diamond palisade.

There with pearls the gates are dight,
  Upon that holy mountain;
And thither come, both day and night,
  Who in the Living Fountain
Have washed their robes from earthly stain
And borne below Christ's lowly chain.

By the hand of the Unknown
  The living stones are moulded
To a glorious shrine, all one,
  Full soon to be unfolded—
The building wherein God doth dwell,
The holy church invisible.

Celestial Jerusalem.

FROM THE LATIN OF BERNARD.

To thee, O dear, dear country,
  Mine eyes their vigils keep;
For very love, beholding
  Thy happy name, they weep.
The mention of thy glory
  Is unction to the breast,
And medicine in sickness,
  And love, and life, and rest.

Brief life is here our portion,
  Brief sorrow, short-lived care;
The life that knows no ending,
  The tearless life, is there.
O one — O only mansion!
  O Paradise of joy!
Where tears are ever banished,
  And joys have no alloy.

Beside thy living waters
  All plants are, great and small, —
The cedar of the forest,
  The hyssop on the wall.
Thy ageless walls are bounded
  With amethyst unpriced;
The saints built up its fabric,
  And the corner-stone is Christ.

Thou hast no shore, fair ocean,
  Thou hast no time, bright day,
Dear fountain of refreshment
  To pilgrims far away.
Upon the Rock of Ages
  They raise the holy tower;
Thine is the victor's laurel,
  And thine the golden dower.

They stand, those halls of Zion,
  Conjubilant with song,
And bright with many an angel,
  And many a martyr throng.
The Prince is ever in them,
  The light is aye serene;
The pastures of the blessed
Are decked in glorious sheen.

There is the throne of David,
  And there, from toil released,
The shout of them that triumph,
  The song of them that feast;
And they beneath their Leader,
  Who conquered in the fight,
Forever and forever
  Are clad in robes of white.

The New Jerusalem.

O MOTHER dear, Jerusalem,
  When shall I come to thee?
When shall my sorrows have an end,
  Thy joys when shall I see?
O happy harbor of God's saints!
  O sweet and pleasant soil!
In thee no sorrow may be found,
  No grief, no care, no toil!

In thee no sickness is at all,
  No hurt, nor any sore;
There is no death, nor ugly sight,
  But life for evermore.
No dimmish clouds o'ershadow thee,
  No dull nor darksome night;
But every soul shines as the sun,
  For God himself gives light.

There lust nor lucre cannot dwell,
  There envy bears no sway;
There is no hunger, thirst, nor heat,
  But pleasure every way.
Jerusalem! Jerusalem!
  Would God I were in thee!
Oh that my sorrows had an end,
  Thy joys that I might see!

No pains, no pangs, no grieving grief,
  No woful wight is there;
No sigh, no sob, no cry is heard,
  No well-away, no fear.
Jerusalem the city is
  Of God our King alone;
The Lamb of God, the light thereof,
  Sits there upon his throne.

Ah, God, that I Jerusalem
  With speed may go behold!
For why? The pleasures there abound
  With tongue cannot be told.
Thy turrets and thy pinnacles
  With carbuncles do shine;
With jasper, pearl, and chrysolite,
  Surpassing pure and fine.

Thy houses are of ivory,
  Thy windows crystal clear,
Thy streets are laid with beaten gold,
  Where angels do appear;
Thy walls are made of precious stones,
  Thy bulwarks diamonds square,
Thy gates are made of orient pearl, —
  O God! if I were there!

Within thy gates no thing can come
  That is not passing clean;
No spider's web, no dirt, no dust,
  No filth may there be seen.
Jehovah, Lord, now come away,
  And end my grief and plaints;
Take me to thy Jerusalem,
  And place me with thy saints,

Who there are crowned with glory great,
  And see God face to face;
They triumph still, and aye rejoice,—
  Most happy is their case.
But we that are in banishment
  Continually do moan;
We sigh, we mourn, we sob, we weep,
  Perpetually we groan.

Our sweetness mixed is with gall,
  Our pleasure is but pain,
Our joys not worth the looking on,
  Our sorrows aye remain.
But there they live in such delight,
  Such pleasure and such play,
That unto them a thousand years
  Seem but as yesterday.

O my sweet home, Jerusalem!
  Thy joys when shall I see;
Thy King sitting upon his throne,
  And thy felicity?
Thy vineyards and thy orchards,
  So wonderful and fair,
And furnished with trees and fruit
  Most beautiful and rare?

Thy gardens and thy goodly walks
  Continually are green;
There grow such sweet and pleasant flowers
  As nowhere else are seen;
There cinnamon and sugar grow,
  There nard and balm abound;
No tongue can tell, no heart can think,
  The pleasures there abound.

There nectar and ambrosie spring,
  There musk and civet sweet;
There many a fine and dainty drug
  Are trod down under feet.
Quite through the streets with pleasant sound
  The flood of life doth flow,
Upon whose banks on every side
  The trees of life do grow.

These trees each month do yield their fruit,
  For evermore they spring;
And all the nations of the world
  To thee their honors bring.
Jerusalem, God's dwelling-place,
  Full sore long I to see;
Oh that my sorrows had an end,
  That I might dwell in thee!

There David stands with harp in hand,
  As master of the queir;
A thousand times that man were blest
  That might his music hear.
There Mary sings Magnificat,
  With tunes surpassing sweet;
And all the virgins bear their part,
  Singing about her feet.

"Te Deum" doth St. Ambrose sing,
  St. Austin doth the like;
Old Simeon and Zacharie
  Have not their songs to seek.
There Magdalene hath left her moan,
  And cheerfully doth sing
With all blest saints, whose harmony
  Through every street doth ring.

Jerusalem! Jerusalem!
  Thy joys fain would I see;
Come quickly, Lord, and end my grief,
  And take me home to thee.
Oh print thy name in my forehead,
  And take me hence away,
That I may dwell with thee in bliss
  And sing thy praises aye.

Jerusalem, thrice happy seat!
  Jehovah's throne on high,—
O sacred city, queen and wife
  Of Christ eternallie!
O comely queen! with glory clad,
  With honor and degree;
All fair thou art, exceeding bright,
  No spot is there in thee!

I long to see Jerusalem,
  The comfort of us all;
For thou art fair and beautiful,
  None ill can thee befall.
In thee, Jerusalem, I say,
  No darkness dare appear;
No night, no shade, no winter foul,
  No time doth alter there.

No candle needs, no moon to shine,
  No glittering stars to light,
For Christ, the King of righteousness,
  There ever shineth bright.
The Lamb unspotted, white, and pure,
  To thee doth stand in lieu
Of light, so great the glory is
  Thine heavenly King to view.

He is the King of kings beset
  In midst his servants' sight;
And they his happy household all
  Do serve him day and night.
There, there the queir of angels sing,
  There the supernal sort
Of citizens (which hence are rid
  From dangers deep) do sport.

There be the prudent prophets all,
  The apostles six and six,
The glorious martyrs in a row,
  And confessors betwixt.
There doth the crew of righteous men
  And matrons all consist,
Young men and maids that here on earth
  Their pleasures did resist.

The sheep and lambs, that hardly 'scaped
  The snares of death and hell,
Triumph in joy eternally,
  Whereof no tongue can tell;
And though the glory of each one
  Doth differ in degree,
Yet is the joy of all alike
  And common, as we see.

There love and charity doth reign,
  And Christ is all in all,
Whom they most perfectly behold
  In glory spiritual.
They love, they praise, they praise, they love,
  They "Holy, holy," cry;
They neither toil, nor faint, nor end,
  But laud continually.

Oh happy thousand times were I,
  If, after wretched days,
I might, with listening ears, conceive
  Those heavenly songs of praise
Which to the eternal King are sung
  By happy wights above —
By saved souls, and angels sweet
  Who love the God of love!

Oh passing happy were my state,
Might I be worthy found
To wait upon my God and King,
His praises there to sound,
And to enjoy my Christ above,
His favor and his grace,
According to his promise made,
Which here I interlace.

"O Father dear," quoth he, "let them
Which thou hast put of old
To me, be there, where, lo, I am,
My glory to behold,
Which I with thee, before this world
Was laid in perfect wise,
Have had, from whence the fountain great
Of glory doth arise."

Again, "If any man will serve,
Then let him follow me;
For where I am, be thou right sure,
There shall my servant be."
And still, "If any man love me,
Him loves my Father dear;
Him I do love; to him myself
In glory will appear."

Lord, take away my misery,
  That there I may behold,
With thee, in thy Jerusalem,
  What here cannot be told,
And so in Zion see my King,
  My Love, my Lord, my All;
Whom now as in a glass I see,
  There face to face I shall.

Oh blessed are the pure in heart,
  Their Sovereign they shall see!
And the most holy heavenly host,
  Who of his household be.
O Lord, with speed dissolve my bands,
  These gins and fetters strong,
For I have dwelt within the tents
  Of Kedar over-long.

Yet search me, Lord, and find me out;
  Fetch me thy fold unto,
That all thy angels may rejoice
  While all thy will I do.
O mother dear, Jerusalem,
  When shall I come to thee?
When shall my sorrows have an end?
  Thy joys when shall I see?

Yet once again I pray thee, Lord,
To quit me from all strife,
That to thine hill I may attain,
And dwell there all my life;
With cherubims and seraphims,
And holy souls of men,
To sing thy praise, O God of hosts,
Forever, and Amen!

Note. — This hymn, the mother of several more recent ones, was formerly ascribed to David Dickson. It was probably altered and enlarged by him from one yet older, in the early part of the seventeenth century.

The Jerusalem of Prophecy.

WM. COWPER.

Hear what God the Lord hath spoken:
"O my people, faint and few,
Comfortless, afflicted, broken,
Fair abodes I build for you;
Thorns of heartfelt tribulation
Shall no more perplex your ways;
You shall name your walls Salvation,
And your gates shall all be Praise.

"There, like streams that feed the garden,
Pleasures without end shall flow;

For the Lord, your faith rewarding,
All his bounty shall bestow;
Still in undisturbed possession
Peace and righteousness shall reign;
Never shall you feel oppression,
Hear the voice of war again.

"Ye no more your suns descending,
Waning moons no more shall see,
But, your griefs forever ending,
Find eternal noon in me;
God shall rise, and, shining o'er you,
Change to day the gloom of night;
He, the Lord, shall be your glory,
God your everlasting light."

The City of Blessedness.

FROM THE LATIN OF PETER DAMIANI.

In the Fount of life perennial the parched heart its thirst would slake,
And the soul, in flesh imprisoned, longs her prison walls to break,—
Exile, seeking, sighing, yearning, in her fatherland to wake.

When with cares oppressed and sorrows, only groans her
grief can tell;
Then she contemplates the glory which she lost when first
she fell;
Present evil but the memory of the vanished good can
swell.

Who can utter what the pleasures and the peace unbroken are,
Where arise the pearly mansions, shedding silvery light
afar,
Festive seats and golden roofs which glitter like the evening star!

Wholly of fair stones most precious are those radiant
structures made;
With pure gold, like glass transparent, are those shining
streets inlaid;
Nothing that defiles can enter, nothing that can soil or
fade.

Stormy winter, burning summer, rage within those regions never,
But perpetual bloom of roses, and unfading spring forever;
Lilies gleam, the crocus glows, and dropping balms their
scents deliver.

Honey pure, and greenest pastures, — this the land of
promise is,
Liquid odors soft distilling, perfumes breathing on the
breeze;
Fruits immortal cluster always on the leafy fadeless
trees.

There no moon shines chill and changing, there no stars
with twinkling ray,
For the Lamb of that blest city is at once the sun and
day;
Night and time are known no longer, day shall never
fade away.

There the saints like suns are radiant, like the sun at
dawn they glow;
Crowned victors after conflict, all their joys together
flow,
And secure they count the battles where they fought the
prostrate foe.

Putting off their mortal vesture, in their Source their
souls they steep;
Truth by actual vision beaming, on its form their gaze
they keep,
Drinking from the living Fountain draughts of living
waters deep.

Time with all its alternations enters not those hosts
among;
Glorious, wakeful, blest, no shade of chance or change
o'er them is flung;
Sickness cannot touch the deathless, nor old age the ever
young.

There their being is eternal; things that cease have ceased
to be;
All corruption there has perished, there they flourish
strong and free;
Thus mortality is swallowed up of life eternally.

Nought from them is hidden, knowing Him to whom all
things are known,
All the spirit's deep recesses, sinless, to each other
shown, —
Unity of will and purpose, heart and mind forever one.

Diverse as their varied labors the rewards to each that
fall,
But Love what she loves in others evermore her own
doth call;
Thus the several joy of each becomes the common joy of
all.

Blessed who the King of heaven in his beauty thus
behold,
And beneath his throne rejoicing see the universe unfold, —
Sun, and moon, and stars, and planets, radiant in his
light unrolled!

Christ, the Palm of faithful victors! of that city make
me free;
When my warfare shall be ended, to its mansions lead
thou me;
Grant me, with its happy inmates, sharer of thy gifts
to be!

Glorious Zion.

FROM THE FRENCH — "HEURES CHRETIENNES DES EGLISES LUTHERIENNES."

'Tis God's decree that all shall die. —
This earth is not my home;
My native land is far on high,
Beyond the starry dome.
I ne'er can reach the heavenly sphere,
To gain the heavenly crown,
Until in vile corruption here
I've laid my body down.

O Thou to whom all worlds pertain,
From earth thou callest me;
And gladly I, through sickness, pain,
And death, shall come to thee.
My trust and hope, O Heavenly Sire,
On thee I still repose;
Do thou, through Christ, when I expire,
Thy bliss to me disclose.

How vast the love of Christ, who came
To die for men below,
And underwent the cross's shame,
That I may 'scape from woe!
His death's to me the source of life,
And where he's now on high,
Afar from death, and sin, and strife,
A home obtain shall I.

My heart's already there; I long
To quit my fleshly load,
To leave these scenes of grief and wrong,
And reach the blessed abode.
There pleasure reigns, and jubilee,
And mighty choirs proclaim,
"Jehovah's holy—holy he,
And holy, too, his name."

'Tis there that all the ancient sires,
  Apostles, saints, and seers,
Exult in songs which love inspires,
  And God in favor hears.
There's naught but triumph, naught but song;
  With plaudits ring the skies —
To Christ, they cry, our joys belong,
  To Christ our anthems rise.

O glorious Zion! thou who far
  In heaven hast reared thy walls,
All bliss is thine; nor want, nor war,
  Nor sickness thee befalls;
Thrice happy they who now thy day
  Of bliss and glory see!
Oh, when shall dawn the blissful ray
  That lights my feet to thee?

I see it come, it now is nigh;
  The moment hastes apace
When Jesus in the lofty sky
  Shall give my soul a place.
And now shall I the crown obtain
  Which waits his folk on high;
Receive me, Lord; now let me reign
  With thee in th' azure sky.

Farewell to kin and friends, farewell
  To all whom here I love;
I now depart, and go to dwell
  With God and saints above.
And now, my kin, my friends, be true
  To God and duty here,
That when to earth ye bid adieu,
  In heaven ye may appear.

Beautiful Zion.

Beautiful Zion! city renowned!
Through the universe wide thy praise shall resound
When straight from thy God thou descendest, the bride,
For thy husband in garments of glory arrayed;
Oh glorious thy beauty, by prophets foretold,
Thy gates of fair pearls, thy streets of pure gold!
To dwell in the city mine may it be —
The beautiful city, Zion the free!

Beautiful Zion! the hope of thy rest
Is a balm for the weary and sorrow-bound breast;
From the bars of affliction, and struggling with sighs,
Sweet prayers for thy coming in breathings arise;

Eternal the joys in thy palaces found;
Forever the song of the saved shall resound;
To dwell in the city mine may it be—
The beautiful city, Zion the free.

Beautiful Zion! desire of the earth!
No sorrow nor sighing in thee shall have birth;
Prisoners of hope, here with burdens oppressed,
How long they to enter thy portals of rest!
Thy rivers of pleasure eternally roll,
Anointing with gladness each blood-ransomed soul:
To dwell in the city mine may it be—
The beautiful city Zion the free!

III. THE PLACE OF REUNION.

Meet Again.

FROM THE GERMAN, BY J. MONTGOMERY.

JOYFUL words, — we meet again!
 Love's own language, comfort darting
 Through the souls of friends at parting!
Life in death — we meet again!

While we walk this vale of tears,
 Compassed round with care and sorrow,
 Gloom to-day and storm to-morrow,
"Meet again" our bosom cheers.

Far in exile when we roam,
 O'er our lost endearments weeping,
 Lonely, silent vigils keeping,
"Meet again" transports us home.

When this weary world is past,
 Happy they whose spirits soaring,
 Vast eternity exploring,
"Meet again" in heaven at last.

Shall we Meet?

H. HARBAUGH.

Oft weeping memory sits alone
Beside some grave at even,
And calls upon some spirit flown;
Oh say, shall those on earth our own
Be ours again in heaven?

Amid these lone sepulchral shades,
Where sleep our dear ones riven,
Is not some lingering spirit near
To tell if those divided here
Unite and know in heaven?

Shall friends who o'er the waste of life
By the same storms are driven,—
Shall they recount in realms of bliss
The fortunes and the tears of this,
And love again in heaven?

When hearts which have on earth been one
By ruthless death are riven,
Why does the one which death has reft
Drag off in grief the one that's left,
If not to meet in heaven?

The warmest love on earth is still
  Imperfect when 'tis given;
But there's a purer clime above,
Where perfect hearts in perfect love
  Unite, and this is heaven.

If love on earth is but "in part,"
  As light and shade at even,
If sin doth plant a thorn between
The truest hearts, there is, I ween,
  A perfect love in heaven.

O happy world! O glorious place,
  Where all who are forgiven
Shall find their loved and lost below,
And hearts, like meeting streams, shall flow,
  Forever one in heaven!

Place of Meeting.

H. BONAR.

'Tis thus they press the hand and part;
  Thus have they bid farewell again;
Yet still they commune, heart with heart,
  Linked by a never-broken chain;—

Still one in life and one in death,
One in their hope of rest above,
One in their joy, their trust, their faith,
One in each other's faithful love.

Yet must they part, and, parting, weep;
What else has earth for them in store?
These farewell pangs, how sharp and deep;
These farewell words, how sad and sore!

Yet shall they meet again in peace,
To sing the song of festal joy,
Where none shall bid their gladness cease,
And none their fellowship destroy;

Where none shall beckon them away,
Nor bid their festival be done;
Their meeting-time the eternal day,
Their meeting-place the eternal throne.

There, hand in hand, firm linked at last,
And heart to heart enfolded all,
They'll smile upon the troubled past,
And wonder why they wept at all.

Then let them press the hand and part,
The dearly loved, the fondly loving,
Still, still, in spirit and in heart,
The undivided, unremoving.

Not Lost, but Gone Before.

SAY, why should friendship grieve for those
 Who safe arrive on Canaan's shore?
Released from all their hurtful foes,
 They are not lost, but gone before.

How many painful days on earth
 Their fainting spirits numbered o'er!
Now they enjoy a heavenly birth;
 They are not lost, but gone before.

Dear is the spot where Christians sleep,
 And sweet the strain which angels pour;
Oh why should we in anguish weep?
 They are not lost, but gone before.

Secure from every mortal care,
 By sin and sorrow vexed no more,
Eternal happiness they share
 Who are not lost, but gone before.

To Zion's peaceful courts above
 In faith triumphant may we soar,
Embracing in the arms of love
 The friends not lost, but gone before.

On Jordan's bank, whene'er we come,
  And hear the swelling waters roar,
Father, convey us safely home
  To friends not lost, but gone before.

Soon with Thee.

FROM THE GERMAN OF J. LANGE.

Our beloved have departed,
While we tarry, broken-hearted,
  In the dreary, empty house;
They have ended life's brief story;
They have reached the home of glory,
  Over death victorious!

Hush that sobbing; weep more lightly;
On we travel, daily, nightly,
  To the rest that they have found;
Are we not upon the river,
Sailing fast to meet forever
  On more holy, happy ground?

Whilst with bitter tears we're mourning,
Thought to buried loves returning,
  Time is hasting us along,
Downward to the grave's dark dwelling,
Upward to the fountain welling
  With eternal life and song!

See ye not the breezes hieing,
Clouds along in hurry flying?
  But we haste more swiftly on,
Ever changing our position,
Ever tossed in strange transition,
  Here to-day, to-morrow gone.

Every hour that passes o'er us
Speaks of comfort yet before us,
  Of our journey's rapid rate;
And, like passing vesper bells,
The clock of time its chiming tells
  At eternity's broad gate.

On we haste to home invited,
There with friends to be united
  In a surer bond than here,
Meeting soon, and met forever;
Glorious hope! forsake us never,
  For thy glimmering light is dear.

Ah, the way is shining clearer,
As we journey, ever nearer
  To the everlasting home;
Friends who there await our landing,
Comrades round the throne now standing,
  We salute you, and we come!

Unity of Saints.

CHARLES WESLEY.

COME, let us join our friends above
  That have obtained the prize,
And on the eagle wings of love
  To joys celestial rise;
Let all the saints terrestrial sing
  With those to glory gone,
For all the servants of our King
  In earth and heaven are one.

One family we dwell in him,
  One church above, beneath,
Though now divided by the stream, —
  The narrow stream of death;
One army of the living God,
  To his command we bow;
Part of his host have crossed the flood,
  And part are crossing now.

Ten thousand to their endless home
  This solemn moment fly;
And we are to the margin come,
  And we expect to die;
His militant, embodied host,
  With wishful looks we stand,
And long to see that happy coast
  And reach the heavenly land.

Our old companions in distress
We haste again to see,
And eager long for our release
And full felicity;
Even now by faith we join our hands
With those that went before,
And greet the blood-besprinkled bands
On the eternal shore.

Our spirits, too, shall quickly join,
Like theirs, with glory crowned,
And shout to see our Captain's sign,
To hear his trumpet sound;
Oh that we now might grasp our Guide!
Oh that the word were given!
Come, Lord of hosts, the waves divide,
And land us all in heaven!

Hallelujah.

FROM THE GERMAN OF M. A. ZILLE.

Meet again! yes, we shall meet again,
Though now we part in pain;
His people all
Together Christ shall call —
Hallelujah!

Soon the days of absence shall be o'er,
And thou shalt weep no more;
Our meeting-day
Shall wipe all tears away —
Hallelujah!

Now I go with gladness to our home,
With gladness thou shalt come;
There I will wait
To meet thee at heaven's gate —
Hallelujah!

Dearest, what delight again to share
Our sweet communion there —
To walk among
The holy ransomed throng —
Hallelujah!

Here, in many a grief, our hearts were one,
But there in joys alone;
Joy fading never,
Increasing, deepening ever —
Hallelujah!

Not to mortal sight can it be given
To know the bliss of heaven;
But thou shalt be
Soon there, and sing with me,
Hallelujah!

Meet again! yes, we shall meet again,
Though now we part in pain;
Together all
His people Christ shall call —
Hallelujah!

At Home Again.

CHRISTIAN EXAMINER.

The earth, all light and loveliness in summer's golden hours,
Smiles in her bridal vesture clad, and crowned with festal flowers
So radiantly beautiful, so like to heaven above,
We scarce can deem more fair that world of perfect bliss and love.

Is this a shadow faint and dim of that which is to come?
What shall the unveiled glories be of our celestial home,
Where waves the glorious tree of life, where streams of bliss gush free,
And all is glowing in the light of immortality!

To see again the home of youth, when weary years have passed,
Serenely bright as when we turned and looked upon it last,

To hear the voice of love, to meet the rapturous embrace,
To gaze through tears of gladness on each dear familiar face, —

Oh! this indeed is joy, though here we meet again to part;
But what transporting bliss awaits the pure and faithful heart,
Where it shall find the loved and lost, those who have gone before,
Where every tear is wiped away, where partings are no more!

When, on devotion's seraph wings, the spirit soars above,
And feels thy presence, Father, Friend, God of eternal love —
Joys of the earth, ye fade away before that living ray
Which gives to the rapt soul a glimpse of pure and perfect day, —

A gleam of heaven's own light, though now its brightness scarce appears
Through the dim shadows which are spread around this vale of tears;
But thine unclouded smile, O God, fills all that glorious place,
Where we shall know as we are known, and see thee face to face!

Recognition.

BISHOP MANT.

SHALL I e'er again thy features trace,
Beloved friend, thy lineaments review?
Yes; though the sunken eye and livid hue,
And lips compressed, have quenched each lively grace,—
Death's triumph; still I recognize the face
Which thine for many a year affection knew;
And what forbids that, clothed with life anew,
It still on memory's tablet holds its place?
Though then thy cheek with deathless bloom be sheen,
And rays of splendor wreathe thy sunlike brow,
That change I deem shall sever not between
Thee and thy former self, nor disallow
That love's tried eyes discern thee through the screen
Of glory then, as of corruption now.

My Dear Companion.

W. C. BRYANT.

How shall I know thee in the sphere which keeps
The disembodied spirits of the dead,
When all of thee that time could wither sleeps
And perishes among the dust we tread?

For I shall feel the sting of ceaseless pain
  If there I meet thy gentle presence not,
Nor hear the voice I love, nor read again
  In thy serenest eyes the tender thought.

Will not thy own meek heart demand me there,
  That heart whose fondest throbs to me were given?
My name on earth was ever in thy prayer,
  Shall it be banished from thy tongue in heaven?

In meadows fanned by heaven's life-breathing wind,
  In the resplendence of that glorious sphere,
And larger movements of the unfettered mind,
  Wilt thou forget the love that joined us here?

The love that lived through all the stormy past,
  And meekly with my harsher nature bore,
And deeper grew, and tenderer to the last,
  Shall it expire with life and be no more?

A happier lot than mine, and larger light,
  Awaits thee there; for thou hast bowed thy will
In cheerful homage to the rule of right,
  And lovest all, and renderest good for ill.

For me, the sordid cares in which I dwell
  Shrink and consume the heart, as heat the scroll:
And wrath has left its scar, — that fire of hell, —
  Has left its frightful scar upon my soul.

Yet, though thou wear'st the glory of the sky,
  Wilt thou not keep the same beloved name,
The same fair, thoughtful brow, and gentle eye,
  Lovelier in heaven's sweet climate, yet the same?

Shalt thou not teach me, in that calmer home,
  The wisdom that I learned so ill in this, —
The wisdom which is love, — till I become
  Thy fit companion in that land of bliss?

Brother, we shall Meet and Rest.

H. BONAR.

Where the faded flower shall freshen, —
  Freshen never more to fade;
Where the shaded sky shall brighten, —
  Brighten never more to shade;
Where the sun-blaze never scorches;
  Where the star-beams cease to chill;
Where no tempest stirs the echoes
  Of the wood, or wave, or hill;
Where the morn shall wake in gladness,
  And the noon the joy prolong,
Where the daylight dies in fragrance,
  Mid the burst of holy song, —
    Brother, we shall meet and rest,
    Mid the holy and the blest!

Where no shadow shall bewilder;
  Where life's vain parade is o'er;
Where the sleep of sin is broken,
  And the dreamer dreams no more;
Where the bond is never severed, —
  Partings, claspings, sob, and moan,
Midnight waking, twilight weeping,
  Heavy noon-tide, — all are done;
Where the child has found its mother,
  Where the mother finds the child;
Where dear families are gathered,
  That were scattered on the wild, —
    Brother, we shall meet and rest,
    Mid the holy and the blest!

Where the hidden wound is healed;
  Where the blighted life re-blooms;
Where the smitten heart the freshness
  Of its buoyant youth resumes;
Where the love that here we lavish
  On the withering leaves of time
Shall have fadeless flowers to fix on,
  In an ever spring-bright clime;
Where we find the joy of loving
  As we never loved before, —
Loving on, unchilled, unhindered,
  Loving once and evermore, —
    Brother, we shall meet and rest,
    Mid the holy and the blest!

Where a blasted world shall brighten
  Underneath a bluer sphere,
And a softer, gentler sunshine
  Shed its healing splendor here;
Where earth's barren vales shall blossom,
  Putting on her robe of green,
And a purer, fairer Eden
  Be where only wastes have been;
Where a King in kingly glory,
  Such as earth has never known,
Shall assume the righteous sceptre,
  Claim and wear the holy crown,—
    Brother, we shall meet and rest,
    Mid the holy and the blest!

Sister, why Starts the Tear?

SISTER and friend, why starts the tear
That kindred minds, no longer near,
Perhaps no more shall mingle here
                Together?

Ere bowed beneath affliction's rod,
The peaceful paths of life we trod,
And journeyed to the house of God
                Together.

No separate wish our thoughts employed,
No separate care our bliss alloyed;
Ever we sorrowed or enjoyed
Together.

What though no more our souls prepare
The various ills of life to bear,
And every transient joy to share
Together?

We have a fairer home on high,—
Dimly its bliss we here descry,—
Where we shall spend eternity
Together.

And where unbroken friendship reigns,
Nor of divided joys complains,
Shall rise our sweet angelic strains
Together.

IV. OUR REST.

There Remaineth a Rest.

FROM THE GERMAN, BY MISS WINKWORTH.

YES, there remaineth yet a rest;
Arise, sad heart, that darkly pines,
By heavy care and pain oppressed,
On whom no sun of gladness shines;
Look to the Lamb! in yon bright fields
Thou'lt know the joy his presence yields;
Cast off thy load and thither haste;
Soon shalt thou fight and bleed no more,
Soon, soon thy weary course be o'er,
And deep the rest thou then shalt taste.

The rest appointed thee of God,
The rest that nought shall break or move,
That ere this earth by man was trod
Was set apart for thee by Love,—
Our Saviour gave his life to win
This rest for thee; oh, enter in!

Hear how his voice sounds far and wide!
  "Ye weary souls, no more delay;
  Loiter not faithless by the way;
Here in my peace and rest abide!"

Ye heavy-laden, come to Him!
  Ye who are bent with many a load,
Come from your prisons drear and dim;
  Toil not thus sadly on your road!
Ye've borne the burden of the day,
And hear ye not your Saviour say,
"I am your refuge and your rest"?
  His children ye, of heavenly birth,
  Howe'er may rage sin, hell, or earth,
Here are ye safe, here calmly blest.

Yonder in joy the sheaves we bring,
  Whose seed was sown on earth in tears;
There in our Father's house we sing
  The song too sweet for mortal ears;
Sorrow and sighing all are past,
And pain and death are fled at last;
There with the Lamb of God we dwell;
  He leads us to the crystal river;
  He wipes away all tears forever;
What there is ours no tongue can tell.

Hunger nor thirst can pain us there;
The time of recompense is come;
Nor cold, nor scorching heat we bear,
Safe sheltered in our Saviour's home;
The Lamb is in the midst, and those
Who followed him through shame and woes
Are crowned with honor, joy and peace;
The dry bones gather life again;
One Sabbath over all shall reign,
Wherein all toil and labor cease.

There is untroubled calm and light;
No gnawing care shall mar our rest;
Ye weary, heed this word aright;
Come, lean upon your Saviour's breast!
Fain would I linger here no more,
Fain to yon happier world upsoar,
And join that bright expectant band!
Oh raise, my soul, the joyful song
That rings through yon triumphant throng;
Thy perfect rest is nigh at hand!

In Heaven alone is Rest.

NOT in this weary world of ours
Can perfect rest be found;
Thorns mingle with its fairest flowers,
Even on cultured ground.

A brook to drink of by the way,
  A rock its shade to cast,
May cheer our path from day to day,
  But such not long can last;
Earth's pilgrim still his loins must gird
  To seek a lot more blest;
And this must be his onward word,—
  "In heaven alone is rest."

This cannot be our resting-place,
  Though now and then a gleam
Of lovely nature, heavenly grace,
  May on thee briefly beam;
Grief's pelting shower, care's darkening shroud,
  Still falls, or hovers near;
And sin's pollutions often cloud
  The light of life while here;
Nor till it "shuffle off the coil"
  In which it lies depressed,
Can the pure spirit cease from toil:
  "In heaven alone is rest;"—

Rest to the weary, anxious soul,
  That on life's toilsome road
Bears onward to the destined goal
  Its heavy, galling load;
Rest unto eyes that often weep
  Beneath the day's broad light,

Or oftener painful vigils keep
  Through the dark hours of night;
But let us bear with pain and care,
  As ills to be redressed,
Relying on the promise fair, —
  "In heaven there will be rest."

Perfect Rest.

Sweet is the name of rest;
  How much the word conveys!
It is to be supremely blest
  In the bright world of praise.

It is to rest from sin,
  Which here will still endure;
The holy place to enter in,
  And be forever pure.

It is to rest from pain,
  From grief, from doubt, from fear;
No sickness, parting, death again,
  Nor any falling tear.

It is to rest with Him
  Whom now unseen we trust,
With cherubim and seraphim,
  And spirits of the just;

A perfect cloudless rest,
An endless Sabbath day,
Blessed portion yet to be possessed,
And never fade away!

I am Weary.

S. ROBERTS.

My feet are worn and weary with the march
Over rough roads and up the steep hill-side;
Oh, city of our God! I fain would see
Thy pastures green, where peaceful waters glide.

My hands are weary, laboring, toiling on,
Day after day, for perishable meat;
Oh, city of our God! I fain would rest;
I sigh to gain thy glorious mercy-seat.

My garments, travel-worn and stained with dust,
Oft rent by briers and thorns that crowd my way,
Would fain be made, O Lord, my righteousness,
Spotless and white in heaven's unclouded ray.

My eyes are weary looking at the sin,
Impiety, and scorn, upon the earth;
Oh, city of our God! within thy walls
All, all are clothed upon with the new birth.

My heart is weary of its own deep sin,
  Sinning, repenting, sinning still alway;
When shall my soul thy glorious presence feel,
  And find its guilt, dear Saviour, washed away?

Patience, poor soul; the Saviour's feet were worn,
  The Saviour's heart and hands were weary, too,
His garments stained, and travel-worn, and old,
  His sacred eyes blinded with tears for you.

Love thou the path of sorrow that he trod;
  Toil on, and wait in patience for thy rest;
Oh, city of our God! we soon shall see
  Thy glorious walls, home of the loved and blest!

I would Fly Away.

WEIR.

Oh, had I wings like yonder bird,
  That soars above its downy nest,
I'd fly away, unseen, unheard,
  Where I might be for aye at rest.

I would not seek these fragrant bowers
  Which bloom beneath a cloudless sky,
Nor could I rest amidst the flowers
  That deck the groves of Araby.

I'd fly, but not to scenes below,
  Though ripe with every promised bliss;
For what's the world? a garnished show,
  A decorated wilderness.

Oh, I would fly and be at rest,
  Far, far beyond each glittering sphere
That hangs upon the azure breast
  Of all we know of heaven here.

And there I'd rest, amidst the joys
  Angelic lips alone can tell,
Where bloom the bowers of Paradise,
  Where songs in sweetest transports swell.

There would I rest, beneath that throne
  Whose glorious circle gilds the sky,
Where sits Jehovah, who alone
  Can wipe the mourner's weeping eye.

When shall I be at Rest?

CHURCH OF ENGLAND QUARTERLY.

WHEN shall I be at rest? my trembling heart
  Grows weary of its burden, sickening still
  With hope deferred; Oh that it were thy will
To loose my bonds and take me where Thou art!

When shall I be at rest? My eyes grow dim
With straining through the gloom; I scarce can see
The waymarks that my Saviour left for me;
Would it were morn and I were safe with him!

When shall I be at rest? Hand over hand
I grasp and climb an ever steeper hill,
A rougher path; Oh that it were thy will
My tired feet might tread the promised land!

Oh that I were at rest! a thousand fears
Come thronging o'er me lest I fail at last;
Would I were safe, all toil and danger past,
And thine own hand might wipe away my tears!

Oh that I were at rest like some I love,
Whose last fond looks drew half my life away,
Seeming to plead that either they might stay
With me on earth, or I with them above!

But why these murmurs? thou didst never shrink
From any toil or weariness for me,—
Not even from that last deep agony;
Shall I beneath my little trials sink?

No, Lord, for when I am indeed at rest,
One taste of that deep bliss will quite efface
The sternest memories of my earthly race,
Save but to swell the sense of being blest.

Then lay on me whatever cross I need
  To bring me there; I know thou canst not be
  Unkind, unfaithful, or untrue to me:
Shall I not toil for thee, when thou for me didst
    bleed?

Rest, Sweetly Rest.

REST, weary soul;
The penalty is borne, the ransom paid,
For all thy sins full satisfaction made;
Strive not thyself to do what Christ has done;
Take the free gift, and make the joys thine own;
No more by pangs of guilt and fear to sin distressed,
Rest, sweetly rest.

Rest, weary heart,
From all thy silent griefs and secret pain,
Thy profitless regrets and longings vain;
Wisdom and love have ordered all the past;
All shall be light and blessedness at last;
Cast off the cares that have so long oppressed,—
Rest, sweetly rest.

Rest, weary head;
Lie down to slumber in the peaceful tomb;
Light from above has broken through its gloom;

Here, in the place where once thy Saviour lay,
Where he shall wake thee on a future day,—
Like a tired child upon its mother's breast,
Rest, sweetly rest.

Rest, spirit free,
In the green pasture of the heavenly shore,
Where sin and sorrow can approach no more;
With all the flock by the Good Shepherd fed,
Beside the streams of life eternal led,
Forever with thy God and Saviour blest,
Rest, sweetly rest.

The Weary are at Rest.

H. H. MILMAN.

Brother, thou art gone before us,
And thy saintly soul is flown
Where tears are wiped from every eye,
And sorrow is unknown;
From the burthen of the flesh,
And from care and fear released,
Where the wicked cease from troubling,
And the weary are at rest.

The toilsome way thou'st travelled o'er,
  And borne the heavy load;
But Christ hath taught thy languid feet
  To reach his blest abode.
Thou'rt sleeping now, like Lazarus
  Upon his father's breast,
Where the wicked cease from troubling,
  And the weary are at rest.

Sin can never taint thee now,
  Nor doubt thy faith assail,
Nor thy meek trust in Jesus Christ
  And the Holy Spirit fail;
And there thou'rt sure to meet the good,
  Whom on earth thou lovedst best,
Where the wicked cease from troubling,
  And the weary are at rest.

"Earth to earth," and "dust to dust,"
  The solemn priest hath said;
So we lay the turf above thee now,
  And we seal thy narrow bed;
But thy spirit, brother, soars away
  Among the faithful blest,
Where the wicked cease from troubling,
  And the weary are at rest.

And when the Lord shall summon us
  Whom thou hast left behind,
May we, untainted by the world,
  As sure a welcome find;
May each, like thee, depart in peace,
  To be a glorious guest
Where the wicked cease from troubling,
  And the weary are at rest.

III.

Who are in Heaven?

WHO ARE IN HEAVEN?

I. OUR GOD.

Whom have I in Heaven but Thee?

SIR ROBERT GRANT.

LORD of earth! thy bounteous hand
Well this glorious frame has planned;
Woods that wave, and hills that tower,
Ocean rolling in his power, —
All that strikes the gaze unsought,
All that charms the lonely thought, —
Friendship — gem transcending price,
Love — a flower from Paradise;
Yet, amid this scene so fair,
Should I cease thy smile to share,
What were all its joys to me?
"Whom have I in heaven but thee?"

Lord of heaven! beyond our sight
Rolls a world of purer light;
There, in love's unclouded reign,
Parted hands shall join again;
Martyrs there, and prophets high,
Blaze, a glorious company,
While immortal music rings
From unnumbered seraph strings;
Oh, that scene is passing fair!
Yet, should'st thou be absent there,
What were all its joys to me?
"Whom have I in heaven but thee?"

Lord of earth and heaven! my breast
Seeks in thee its only rest;
I was lost — thy accents mild
Homeward lured thy wandering child;
I was blind — thy healing ray
Charmed the long eclipse away;
Source of every joy I know,
Solace of my every woe;
Yet should once thy smile divine
Cease upon my soul to shine,
What were heaven or earth to me?
"Whom have I in heaven but thee?"

Dwelling in Light.

EDMUND SPENSER.

His sceptre is the rod of Righteousnesse,
With which He bruseth all His foes to dust,
And the great dragon strongly doth represse,
Under the rigour of His iudgment iust;
His seate is Truth, to which the faithfull trust,
From whence proceed her beames so pure and bright,
That all about Him sheddeth glorious light.

But that immortall light which there doth shine
Is many thousand times more bright, more cleare,
More excellent, more glorious, more divine,
Through which to God all mortall actions here,
And even the thoughts of men, do plaine appeare;
For from th' Eternall Truth it doth proceed,
Through heavenly vertue which her beames doe breed.

With the great glorie of that wondrous light
His throne is all encompassed around,
And hid in his owne brightnesse from the sight
Of all that look thereon with eyes unsound;
And underneath his feet are to be found
Thunder, and lightning, and tempestuous fyre,
The instruments of his avenging yre.

There, in his bosome, Sapience doth sit,
  The soveraine dearling of the Deity,
Clad like a queene, in royall robes most fit
  For so great powre and peerelesse majesty,
  And all with gemmes and iewels gorgeously
Adorned, that brighter then the starres appeare,
And make her native brightnesse seem more cleare.

And on her head a crown of purest gold
  Is set, in signe of highest soverainty;
And in her hand a scepter she doth hold,
  With which she rules the house of God on hy,
  And menageth the ever-moving sky,
And in the same these lower creatures all
Subiected to her powre imperiall.

In thy Light shall we see Light.

FROM THE ITALIAN OF DANTE, BY I. C. WRIGHT.

A LIGHT there is above which plainly shows
  The great Creator to the creature, who
In seeing him alone can find repose,
And in a circle spreads to such degree,
  That for the sun would its circumference
A girdle of too great dimensions be;

All its appearance one vast ray of light
  Reflected from the swiftest heaven, which thence
Derives both its existence and its might.
And as a cliff looks down upon the bed
  Of some clear stream, to see how richly crowned
With flowers and foliage is its lofty head,
So, all from earth who hither e'er returned,
  Seated on more than thousand thrones around,
Within the Eternal Light themselves discerned;
And if the very lowest tier receives
  A light so great, how wonderful must be
This rose expanded in its utmost leaves!

God in His Temple.

I. WATTS.

LORD of the worlds above,
  How pleasant and how fair
The dwellings of thy love,
  Thy earthly temples, are;
    To thine abode
    My heart aspires,
    With warm desires
    To see my God.

The sparrow for her young
  With pleasure seeks her nest,
And wandering swallows long
  To find their wonted rest;
    My spirit faints,
    With equal zeal
    To rise and dwell
    Among thy saints.

Oh happy souls that pray
  Where God appoints to hear;
Oh happy men that pay
  Their constant service there;
    They praise thee still,
    And happy they
    That love the way
    To Zion's hill.

They go from strength to strength,
  Through this dark vale of tears,
Till each arrives at length,
  Till each in heaven appears.
    Oh glorious seat,
    When God our King
    Shall thither bring
    Our willing feet.

His Throne.

JEREMY TAYLOR.

O BEAUTEOUS God, uncircumscribed treasure
Of an eternal pleasure!
Thy throne is seated far
Above the highest star,
Where thou prepar'st a glorious place
Within the brightness of thy face
For every spirit
To inherit
That builds his hopes upon thy merit,
And loves thee with a holy charity.
What ravished heart, seraphic tongue, or eyes
Clear as the morning's rise,
Can speak, or think, or see,
That bright eternity,
Where the great King's transparent throne
Is of an entire jasper stone?
There the eye
O' th' chrysolite,
And a sky
Of diamonds, rubies, chrysoprase,
And, above all, thy holy face,
Makes an eternal clarity
When thou thy jewels up dost bind; that day
Remember us, we pray,

That where the beryl lies,
And the crystal, 'bove the skies,
There thou may'st appoint us place
Within the brightness of thy face,
And our soul
In the scroll
Of life and blissfulness enroll,
That we may praise thee to eternity:
Allelujah!

His Throne and Temple.

W. A. MUHLENBERG.

Since o'er thy footstool here below
Such radiant gems are strewn,
Oh what magnificence must glow,
My God, about thy throne!
So brilliant here those drops of light,
Where the full ocean rolls, how bright!

If night's blue curtain of the sky,
With thousand stars inwrought,
Hung like a royal canopy
With glittering diamonds fraught,
Be, Lord, thy temple's outer veil,
What splendor at the shrine must dwell!

The dazzling sun, at noontide hour,
  Forth from his flaming vase
Flinging o'er earth the golden shower
  Till vale and mountain blaze,
But shows, O Lord, one beam of thine;
What, then, the day where thou dost shine!

Ah, how shall these dim eyes endure
  That noon of living rays;
Or how my spirit, so impure,
  Upon thy glory gaze?
Anoint, O Lord, anoint my sight,
And robe me for that world of light.

Open is the Starry Hall.

FROM THE LATIN, BY WILLIAMS.

Open is the starry hall;
Hear ye? 'tis the Bridegroom's call!
Holy virgins, one and all,
    Ready stand,
For the heavenly festival
    Is at hand!

Come at last the nuptial day,
Tears forever passed away;
Fled the prison-house, the clay,
And the thrall;
God forever your sure stay,
And your all!

In his presence is the store,
Purest joys for evermore,
And the fountain flowing o'er;
No more night,
Safe upon the happy shore
Of the light!

What was royalty's short flower,
Or the triumph of an hour?
What fleet pleasure's fading bower
And control?
God's own presence is the dower
Of the soul!

Wondrous, glorious mystery,
When the soul from flesh is free!
Bond of sweetness which shall be
When the heart
Joined is to Deity,
Never to part!

II. OUR SAVIOUR.

The Good Shepherd.

FROM THE SPANISH, BY BRYANT.

REGION of life and light,
Land of the good whose earthly toils are o'er,
Nor frost nor heat may blight
Thy vernal beauty, fertile shore,
Yielding thy blessed fruits for evermore!

There, without crook or sling,
Walks the Good Shepherd; blossoms white and red
Round his meek temples cling;
And to sweet pastures led,
His own loved flock beneath his eye is fed.

He guides, and near him they
Follow delighted; for he makes them go
Where dwells eternal May,
And heavenly roses blow,
Deathless, and gathered but again to grow.

He leads them to the height
Named of the infinite and long-sought Good,
And fountains of delight;
And where his feet have stood
Springs up along the way their tender food.

And when, in the mid skies,
The climbing sun has reached his highest bound,
Reposing as he lies,
With all his flock around,
He witches the still air with numerous sound.

From his sweet lute flow forth
Immortal harmonies, of power to still
All passions born of earth,
And draw the ardent will
Its destiny of goodness to fulfil.

Might but a little part,
A wandering breath, of that high melody
Descend into my heart
And change it, till it be
Transformed and swallowed up, O Love, in thee!

Ah! then my soul should know,
Beloved, where thou liest at noon of day,
And, from this place of woe
Released, should take its way
To mingle with thy flock, and never stray.

Our Shepherd.

FROM THE SPANISH OF LUIS DE LEON, BY GEO. TICKNOR.

AND dost thou, holy Shepherd, leave
Thine unprotected flock alone
Here, in this darksome vale, to grieve,
While thou ascend'st thy glorious throne?

Oh where can they their hopes now turn
Who never lived but on thy love?
Where rest the hearts that for thee burn
When thou art lost in light above?

How shall those eyes now find repose
That turn in vain thy smile to see?
What can they hear save mortal woes
Who lose thy voice's melody?

And who shall lay his tranquil hand
Upon the troubled ocean's might?
Who hush the winds by his command?
Who guide us through this starless night?

For Thou art gone! that cloud so bright,
That bears thee from our love away,
Springs upward through the dazzling light,
And leaves us here to weep and pray!

Christ Arisen.

WM. H. BATHURST.

WHY search ye in the narrow tomb
  For him who lives on high?
Heaven spreads her gates to make him room;
  His glory fills the sky.

Lift up your hearts and stretch your eyes;
  The Saviour is not here;
Behold the Conqueror arise,
  To grace a brighter sphere.

Angels, with loud, exulting songs,
  Welcome their Lord again;
To us the victory belongs;
  For us the Lamb was slain.

And shall we, Lord, ascend with thee,
  And see thee as thou art,
From death's terrific power made free,
  And saved from Satan's dart?

Saviour, since thou art gone before,
  Oh grant that we may go
Where sin's dark empire is no more,
  And death a vanquished foe!

Christ Ascended.

FROM THE LATIN OF BEDE.

A HYMN of glory let us sing!
New hymns throughout the world shall ring;
Christ, by a way none ever trod,
Ascendeth to the throne of God.

The angels say to the eleven,
"Why stand ye gazing into heaven?"
This is the Saviour — this is He!
Jesus hath triumphed gloriously.

They said the Lord should come again,
As these beheld him rising then,
Calm soaring through the radiant sky,
Mounting its dazzling summits high.

May our affections thither tend,
And thither constantly ascend,
Where, seated on the Father's throne,
Thee, reigning in the heavens, we own!

Be thou our present joy, O Lord,
Who wilt be ever our reward;
And, as the countless ages flee,
May all our glory be in thee!

Christ Mindful.

SOFT as falls the heavenly dew,
Weary nature to renew,
Or the flakes, unearthly pure,
Of the snowy coverture;
Thus, too high for mortal sense,
Christ his presence doth dispense,
Seen in diviner sympathies,
In sacred joys that rise
And waft the soul to heaven with rapture's sighs.

Jesus hath left his flock below,
  And gone into the mount to pray
For his poor wanderers, left to go
  Without him on the stormy way;
But when the tempest rageth high
With dread their fearful hearts to try,
Their tearful eyes shall see him nigh,
Stilling the tempest into peace,
Bidding all dark forebodings cease,
Shedding abroad his heavenly love,
Inspiring hopes of joys above,
Where soon upon the blissful shore
They from their Lord shall go on stormy waves
      no more.

Christ the King of Glory.

MADAN.

Hail the day that sees him rise
Ravished from our wistful eyes!
Christ, awhile to mortals given,
Reascends his native heaven;
There the mighty Conqueror waits;
"Lift your heads, eternal gates!
Wide unfold the radiant scene!
Take the King of Glory in!"

Circled round with angel-powers,
Their triumphant Lord and ours,
Conqueror o'er death, hell, and sin, —
Take the King of Glory in;
Him though kindest heaven receives,
Still he loves the earth he leaves;
Though returned to his throne,
Still he calls mankind his own.

See, he lifts his hands above;
See, he shows the prints of love;
Hark! his gracious lips bestow
Blessings on his church below;
Still for us he intercedes;
Prevalent his death he pleads;
Next himself prepares our place,
Saviour of the human race.

"Master," may we ever say,
"Taken from our head to-day,
See thy faithful servants, see,
Ever gazing up to thee!
Grant, though parted from our sight,
High above yon azure height,
Grant our hearts may thither rise,
Seeking thee beyond the skies!"

Ever upward may we move,
Wafted on the wings of love,
Looking when our Lord shall come,
Longing, gasping after home!
There may we with thee remain,
Partners of thine endless reign,
There thy face unclouded see,
Find our heaven of heavens in thee!

Christ the Star.

The last sand from Time's hour-glass
Shall soon disappear,
And like vapor shall vanish
This old-rolling sphere.

Off the floor, like the chaff-stream
  In the dark, windy day,
From the fan of destruction
  Shall suns drift away;

And the meteors of glory,
  Which wilder the wise,
Only gleam till we open
  In true worlds our eyes.

But aloft in God's heaven
  There blazes a Star,
And I live whilst I'm watching
  Its light from afar.

From its lustre immortal
  My soul caught the spark
Which shall beam on undying
  When the sunshine is dark.

So transforming its radiance,
  Its strength so benign,
The dull clay burns a ruby,
  And man grows divine.

To the zenith ascended
  From Joseph's dark tomb,
Star of Jesse! so rivet
  My gaze midst the gloom,

That thy beauty imbibing,
My dross may refine,
And in splendor reflected
I burn and I shine!

Christ the Light.

There walk the saved! yea, they who bore,
While traversing life's stormy shore,
Through tears and blood the hallowed cross,
Who, purged from earth's terrestrial dross,
Received the Saviour's form impressed,
Whose signet on each hallowed breast
Enstamped the mystic name, unknown
To all save those around the throne;

Who, calm 'mid earth's tumultuous strife,
Drew from himself that inward life
Which spirits breathe, from sense apart,
While deep in each devoted heart
The formless glory dwelt serene,
Of old in cherub splendor seen;
Prelude of bliss reserved above,
In perfect light, for perfect love.

Now all in heaven! no temple there
Unfolds its gates; no voice of prayer
From that bright multitude ascends,
But holy rapture reverent bends
Before the mediatorial throne,
Before the Lamb, whose beams alone
Irradiate that eternal sky,
The bursting blaze of Deity!

Soft is the voice of golden lutes;
Sweet bloom heaven's fair, ambrosial fruits;
Bright beams the dazzling lustre, shed
From radiant gems in order spread,
From golden streets, from emerald floors,
From crystal floods, from pearly doors,
From rainbow tints, from angel wings,
From all unuttered glorious things.

Yet not that city's dazzling glow,
Nor limpid water's crystal flow,
Nor dulcet harmony that springs
From golden lyres; no angel wings,
Though glittering with intensest dyes
Reflected from immortal skies,
Complete the palmy bliss of those
For whom heaven's pearly gates unclose.

No; 'tis with unfilmed eyes to see
The once incarnate Deity,
Who still with lamb-like meekness bears,
Imprinted deep, those glorious scars
Whence issued wide that crimson flow
In which their robes were washed below,
Which bought that crown whose splendor bright
Now spheres them in that world of light.

No, 'tis not all that heaven can show
Of great or fair unglimpsed below,
Nor converse deep with spirits high,
Who saw those volleyed lightnings fly
Which scathed their bright compeers in bliss,
And hurled them down to hell's abyss;
Who marked creation rise sublime,
And hymned the early birth of time;—

No, not with minds like these to blend,
And feel each angel form a friend,
But God, their fount, to know and see,
From all-pervading Deity;
To catch the nearer burst of light;
To gain the beatific sight;
Entranced in glory's peerless blaze,
Conformed to him, on him to gaze.

Christ Enthroned.

I. WATTS.

OH the delights, the heavenly joys,
  The glories of the place,
Where Jesus sheds the brightest beams
  Of his o'erflowing grace!

Sweet majesty and awful love
  Sit smiling on his brow,
And all the glorious ranks above
  At humble distance bow.

Princes to his imperial name
  Bend their bright sceptres down;
Dominions, thrones, and powers rejoice
  To see him wear the crown.

Archangels sound his lofty praise
  Through every heavenly street,
And lay their highest honors down
  Submissive at his feet.

Those soft, those blessed feet of his,
  That once rude iron tore,
High on a throne of light they stand
  And all the saints adore.

His head, the dear, majestic head,
  That cruel thorns did wound,
See what immortal glories shine
  And circle it around!

This is the man, th' exalted man,
  Whom we, unseen, adore;
But when our eyes behold his face,
  Our hearts shall love him more.

Lord, how our souls are all on fire
  To see thy blest abode;
Our tongues rejoice in tunes of praise
  To our incarnate God!

And while our faith enjoys this sight,
  We long to leave our clay,
And with thy fiery chariots, Lord,
  To fetch our souls away!

Christ the King.

FROM THE LATIN OF PRUDENTIUS.

YE whoe'er for Christ are seeking,
  Lift your longing eyes on high;
There behold the glory breaking
  Of celestial majesty.

Bright the vision there unveiling,
  With unbounded lustre bright,
High, sublime, and never failing,
  Elder than primeval light.

He is King all realms to gather,
  King whom Israel's tribes obey,
Promised to his people's father,
  Abraham, and his seed for aye.

Seers to him high witness breathing,
  Seal their words with love and fear;
Him th' eternal Sire bequeathing,
  Bids his own believe and hear.

Jesus Adored.

JOHN BAKEWELL.

Hail, thou once despised Jesus!
  Hail, thou Galilean King!
Thou didst suffer to release us,
  Thou didst free salvation bring;
Hail, thou agonizing Saviour,
  Bearer of our sin and shame;
By thy merits we find favor;
  Life is given through thy name!

Paschal Lamb, by God appointed,
  All our sins on thee were laid;
By almighty love anointed,
  Thou hast full atonement made;
All thy people are forgiven,
  Through the virtue of thy blood;
Opened is the gate of heaven;
  Peace is made 'twixt man and God.

Jesus, hail! enthroned in glory,
  There forever to abide;
All the heavenly hosts adore thee,
  Seated at thy Father's side;
There for sinners thou art pleading,
  There thou dost our place prepare,
Ever for us interceding,
  Till in glory we appear.

Worship, honor, power, and blessing,
  Thou art worthy to receive;
Loudest praises, without ceasing,
  Meet it is for us to give;
Help, ye bright, angelic spirits;
  Bring your sweetest, noblest lays;
Help to sing our Saviour's merits,
  Help to chant Immanuel's praise.

Jesus Extolled.

BRYDGES.

Head of the hosts in glory!
We joyfully adore thee,
  Thy church on earth below,
Blending with those on high,
Where, through the azure sky,
Thy saints in ecstasy
  Forever glow.

Then raise the song of gladness,
To dissipate our sadness
  Along this vale of tears;
We wend our weary way
Up to the realms of day,
And watch, and wait, and pray,
  Constant in fears.

Holy apostles, beaming
With radiance brightly streaming
  From diadems of power,
Call on the awful name,
That we, through flood and flame,
The gospel may proclaim
  In every hour.

Martyrs, whose mystic legions
March o'er yon heavenly regions
  In triumph round and round,
Wave, wave your banners, wave!
For Christ, our Saviour, clave
For death itself a grave,
  In hell profound.

Saints, in fair circles casting
Rich trophies everlasting
  At Jesu's pierced feet,
Amidst our rude alarms
Stretch forth your conquering arms,
That we, too, safe from harms,
  In heaven may meet.

Virgins, in bliss transcendent,
Whose coronals resplendent
  Unwithering bloom,
Exalt in ceaseless lays
Him whom all anthems praise,
And oft our spirits raise
  With your perfume.

Angels, archangels, glorious
Guards of the church victorious,
  Sing to the Lamb!

Crown him with crowns of light,
One of the Three by right,
Love, Majesty, and Might,
  The great I AM!

The Prince of Peace.

HENRY VAUGHAN.

My soul, there is a countrie
  Afar beyond the stars,
Where stands a winged sentrie,
  All skilful in the wars.

There, above noise and danger,
  Sweet peace sits crowned with smiles,
And One born in a manger
  Commands the beau'teous files.

He is thy gracious Friend,
  And (O my soul, awake!)
Did in pure love descend
  To die here for thy sake.

If thou canst get but thither,
  There grows the flowre of peace
The rose that cannot wither,
  Thy fortresse and thy ease.

Leave, then, thy foolish ranges,
  For none can thee secure
But One, who never changes,
  Thy God, thy Life, thy Cure.

King, High Priest, Immanuel.

FROM THE GERMAN, BY H. MILLS.

Our Jesus, now at God's right hand,
  Is high in glory seated;
He reigns in that dear father-land,
  From far with transport greeted,
Whither our warm affections move,
And where celestial spirits love
  Him, as their Lord, to honor.

Above all principality
  His shining throne he raises;
The angels' highest minstrelsy
  In vain would reach his praises;
To him the songs of cherubim,
Responded by the seraphim,
  Cry "Holy, holy, holy!"

All things are subject to his reign,
  And earth and skies together,
What is, and what has ever been,
  The upper world and nether;
All power and might of every name
Shall own, dear Lord, thy sovereign claim;
  Thy rule is universal.

Thou must, too, be our great High Priest,
  Thy blood our souls' oblation;
None else can show our guilt released,
  Or bless us with salvation;
The grace we need none else can give,
For none, like thee, a priest shall live
  To intercede forever.

Bright hopes to us thy love affords;
  To faith thou naught deniest;
Thou reignest now the Lord of lords,
  Above all kings the highest;
Thy throne of righteousness secure,
Through endless ages will endure,
  Dispensing grace and judgment.

Immanuel, ever at our side
  Thou'lt be, till time is ended,
Through all our pilgrimage to guide,
  With power and mercy blended;

In every strait wilt bring us through,
For us contend, and conquer, too,
Till Death himself is vanquished!

Thou say'st, "Him that shall overcome
None from my joys shall sever;
A child of God I'll bring him home,
To share my throne forever,
E'en as I, too, have victory won,
And sit upon my Father's throne
In majesty and glory."

The Redeemer and Redeemed.

MRS. ANNE STEELE.

No sun shall gild the blest abode
With his meridian ray,
But the more radiant throne of God
Diffuse eternal day.

Sorrow, and pain, and every care,
And discord, there shall cease,
And perfect joy, and love sincere,
Adorn the realms of peace.

The soul, from sin forever free,
  Shall mourn its power no more,
But, clothed in spotless purity,
  Redeeming love adore.

There, on a throne how dazzling bright,
  Th' exalted Saviour shines,
And beams ineffable delight
  On all the heavenly minds.

There shall the followers of the Lamb
  Join in immortal songs,
And endless honors to his name
  Employ their tuneful tongues.

While sweet reflection calls to mind
  The scenes of mortal care,
When God, their God, forever kind,
  Was present to their prayer;

How will the wonders of his grace
  In their full lustre shine!
His wisdom, power, and faithfulness,
  All-glorious, all-divine!

The Saviour, dying, risen, crowned,
  Shall swell the lofty strains,
Seraph and saint his praise resound
  Through all th' ethereal plains.

But oh, their transports! oh, their songs!
What mortal thought can paint?
Transcendent glory awes our tongues,
And all our notes are faint.

Lord, tune our hearts to praise and love,
Our feeble notes inspire,
Till, in thy blissful courts above,
We join the heavenly choir.

The Sympathizing Brother.

MARIA J. JEWSBURY.

A SOUND in yonder glade,
But not of fount or breeze,
A sound, but not of the whispering made
By the palm and the olive trees;
It is not the minstrel's lute,
Nor the swell of the night-bird's song,
Nor the city's hum, when all else is mute,
By echo borne along.

'Tis a voice, — the Saviour's own, —
"Woman, why weepest thou?"
She turns, and her grief is forever flown,
And the shade that dimmed her brow;

He is there, her risen Lord,
  No more to know decline;
He is there, with peace in his every word,
  The wept one, still divine.

"My Father's throne to share,
  As King, as God, I go;
But a brother's heart will be with me there
  For my brethren left below."
The weeper is laid in dust;
  Her Lord is throned on high;
But ours may be still that weeper's trust,
  And ours that Lord's reply.

Mourner, mid nature's bloom,
  Dimming its light with tears,
And captive, to whom the lone, dark room
  Grows darker yet with fears,
And spirit, that, like a bird,
  Rests not on sea or shore,
The voice in the olive-glade once heard,
  Hear ye, and weep no more.

Our Fellow-Sufferer.

JOHN LOGAN.

Where high the heavenly temple stands,
The house of God not made with hands,
A great High Priest our nature wears,
The Guardian of mankind appears.

Though now ascended up on high,
He bends on earth a brother's eye;
Partaker of the human name,
He knows the frailty of our frame.

Our Fellow-Sufferer yet retains
A fellow-feeling of our pains,
And still remembers, in the skies,
His tears, his agonies, and cries.

In every pang that rends the heart,
The Man of sorrows had a part;
He sympathizes with our grief,
And to the sufferer sends relief.

With boldness, therefore, at the throne
Let us make all our sorrows known,
And ask the aid of heavenly power
To help us in an evil hour.

Yes, for Me, for Me.

H. BONAR.

YES, for me, for me he careth
  With a brother's tender care;
Yes, with me, with me he shareth
  Every burden, every fear.

Yes, o'er me, o'er me he watcheth,
  Ceaseless watcheth, night and day;
Yes, even me, even me he snatcheth
  From the perils of the way.

Yes, for me he standeth pleading
  At the mercy-seat above,
Ever for me interceding,
  Constant in untiring love.

Yes, in me abroad he sheddeth
  Joys unearthly, love and light;
And to cover me he spreadeth
  His paternal wing of night.

Yes, in me, in me he dwelleth,
  I in him, and he in me;
And my empty soul he filleth,
  Here and through eternity.

Thus I wait for his returning,
  Singing all the way to heaven;
Such the joyful song of morning,
  Such the tranquil song of even.

III. HOLY ANGELS.

Cherubim.

FROM THE ITALIAN, BY I. C. WRIGHT.

ARRAYED in semblance of a snow-white rose,
That holy army was revealed to sight,
Which for his spouse in death our Saviour chose.
But the winged cherubs that behold and sing
His praise, whose chords of love to love invite,
And laud the goodness of their heavenly King, —
E'en as a troop of bees now seek the flowers,
And now return with their delicious store,
To lay it up amid their waxen bowers, —
On the vast flower descended from above,
Whence from its numerous leaves again they soar
Back to the realm where ever dwells their Love.
The looks of all were bright with living flame,
With gold their pinions, and their forms so white,

No snow such perfect purity could claim;
  Fanning their plumage, as with wing untired
From round to round they on the flower alight,
  They impart the peace and love they have acquired;
Nor by their rapid passage, as they fly
  Betwixt the Flower and Fountain of their bliss,
Was aught of splendor lost unto mine eye;
  For through the world the Ray divine is sent
Where'er most worthy of that light it is,
  Nought having power to cause impediment
In this blest realm, where spirits of ancient days
  And modern meet, in endless bliss to dwell,
All to one Point their sight and ardors raise.

Song of the Cherubim.*

FROM THE RUSSIAN OF KHERUVIMIJ, BY BOWRING.

SEE the glorious cherubim
  Thronging round the Eternal's throne;
Hark! they sing their holy hymn:
  To the unknown Three in One,
All-supporting Deity,
Living Spirit, praise to thee!

* The hymn chanted in the Russian churches during the procession of the cup.

Rest, ye worldly tumults, rest;
Here let all be peace and joy;
Grief no more shall rend our breast,
Tears no more shall dew our eye.

Heaven-directed spirits, rise
To the temple of the skies!
Join the ranks of angels bright,
Near th' Eternal's dazzling light.
Hallelujah!

Angels and the Glorified.

H. H. MILMAN.

WHAT means yon blaze on high?
The empyrean sky,
Like the rich veil of some proud fane, is rending;
I see the star-paved land
Where all the angels stand,
Even to the highest height in burning rows ascending,
Some with their wings disspread,
And bowed the stately head,
As on some mission of God's love departing,
Like flames from midnight conflagration starting;
Behold! the appointed messengers are they,
And nearest earth they wait to waft our souls away.

Higher and higher still
More lofty statures fill
The jasper courts of the everlasting dwelling;
Cherub and seraph pace
The illimitable space,
While sleep the folded plumes from their white shoulders swelling;
From all the harping throng
Bursts the tumultuous song,
Like the unceasing sound of cataracts pouring,
Hosanna o'er hosanna louder soaring,
That, faintly echoing down to earthly ears,
Hath seemed the concert sweet of the harmonious spheres.

Still my rapt spirit mounts,
And lo! beside the founts
Of flowing light Christ's chosen saints reclining;
Distinct among the blaze
Their palm-crowned heads they raise,
Their white robes e'en through that o'erpowering lustre shining.
Each in his place of state,
Long the bright twelve have sate,
O'er the celestial Zion high uplifted;
While those with deep prophetic raptures gifted,
Where life's glad river rolls its tideless streams,
Enjoy the full completion of their heavenly dreams.

Again, I see again
The great victorious train,
The martyr army from their toils reposing,
The blood-red robes they wear
Empurpling all the air,
Even their immortal limbs the signs of wounds disclosing;
Oh, holy Stephen! thou
Art there, and on thy brow
Hast still the placid smile it wore in dying,
When, under the heaped stones in anguish lying,
Thy clasping hands were fondly spread to heaven,
And thy last accents prayed thy foes might be forgiven.

Beyond, ah! who is there
With the white snowy hair?
'Tis He, 'tis He, the Son of man, appearing
At the right hand of One,
The darkness of whose throne
That sun-eyed host behold with awe and fearing;
O'er him the rainbow springs,
And spreads its emerald wings
Down to the glassy sea, his loftiest seat o'erarching.
Hark! thunders from his throne, like steel-clad armies marching;
The Christ! the Christ commands us to his home!
Jesus, Redeemer, Lord, we come, we come, we come!

Singing Hallelujah.

YE angels, praise the Lord;
His wondrous works proclaim,
At whose creating word
You into being came.
Endowed with strength and holiness,
In realms of everlasting bliss,
Where glory makes the day,
'Tis yours a higher bliss to know,
The Source from whence your blessings flow,
And his commands obey.

Ye heard the voice that bade
Creation spring to light;
Creation rose, displayed
In majesty of might.
Unnumbered worlds in order stood;
God saw the work, pronounced it good,
While all your hosts adored;
Their living harps to praise were strung,
The heavens with hallelujahs rung
To the Creator, Lord.

A higher theme of praise,
A brighter Sun has beamed;
The subject of your lays —
A dying world redeemed;

"Glory to God!" was then your song;
Redemption will the strain prolong
Through all eternity;
Creation's theme may die away
Like stars before the morning ray,
But this can never die.

Your portion is increase
Of love, and bliss, and praise;
The works of God ne'er cease
His attributes to raise.
Oh height of praise in heaven above,
When all the mighty plan of love
Accomplished shall appear;
When, crowned by her Messiah's side,
The church, his purchased, spotless bride,
Shall all your blessings share!

Waiting upon God.

EDMUND SPENSER.

ANGELS bright,
All glistening glorious in their Maker's light;—

To them the heaven's illimitable hight
(Not this round heaven which we from hence behold,
Adorned with thousand lamps of burning light,

And with ten thousand gemmes of shyning gold)
He gave as their inheritance to hold,
That they might serve him in eternall blis,
And be partakers of those ioys of his.

There they in their trinall triplicities
About him wait, and on his will depend,
Either with nimble wings to cut the skies,
When he them on his messages doth send,
Or on his owne dread presence to attend,
Where they behold the glorie of his light,
And caroll hymnes of love both day and night.
Both day and night is unto them all one;
For he his beames doth unto them extend,
That darknesse there appeareth never none;
Ne hath their day, ne hath their blisse an end.
But there their termelesse time in pleasure spend;
Ne ever should their happinesse decay,
Had not they dar'd their Lord to disobay.

Adoring the Lamb.

BRYDGES.

Bright cherubim and seraphim,
In one mysterious crowd,
Expand the everlasting hymn
That rolls from cloud to cloud.

Odors, in folds of fragrant fumes,
Pervade the ravished skies,
Whilst angels form, with arching plumes,
A firmament of eyes.

They gaze, and as they gaze they shine,
And as they shine admire,
With adoration all divine,
All love, all life, all fire.

No temple there is made with hands,
By human priesthood trod;
Alone the once-slain Victim stands,
The living Lamb of God.

Witnesses for Jesus.

PHILIP DODDRIDGE.

O YE immortal throng
Of angels round the throne,
Join with our feeble song
To make the Saviour known;
On earth ye knew
His wondrous grace;
His beauteous face
In heaven ye view.

Ye saw the heaven-born child
  In human flesh arrayed,
Benevolent and mild,
  While in the manger laid;
  And praise to God,
    And peace on earth,
    For such a birth
  Proclaimed aloud.

Ye in the wilderness
  Beheld the tempter spoiled,
Well known in every dress,
  In every combat foiled,
  And joyed to crown
    The Victor's head
    When Satan fled
  Before his frown.

Around the bloody tree
  Ye pressed with strong desire
That wondrous sight to see,
  The Lord of life expire;
  And, could your eyes
    Have known a tear,
    Had dropped it there
  In sad surprise.

Around his sacred tomb
  A willing watch ye keep,
Till the blest moment come
  To rouse him from his sleep;
  Then rolled the stone,
    And all adored
    Your rising Lord
  With joy unknown.

When all arrayed in light
  The shining Conqueror rode,
Ye hailed his rapturous flight
  Up to the throne of God,
  And waved around
    Your golden wings,
    And struck your strings
  Of sweetest sound.

The warbling notes pursue,
  And louder anthems raise,
While mortals sing with you
  Their own Redeemer's praise;
  And thou, my heart,
    With equal flame,
    And joy the same,
  Perform thy part.

Serving the Redeemer.

GREGG.

BEYOND the glittering starry skies,
Far as the eternal hills,
Yon heaven of heavens with living light
Our great Redeemer fills.

Legions of angels, strong and fair,
In countless armies shine,
And swell his praise with golden harps,
Attuned to songs divine.

"Hail, Prince," they cry, "forever hail,
Whose unexampled love
Moved thee to quit those glorious realms
And royalties above!"

While he did condescend on earth
To suffer grief and pain,
They cast their honors at his feet,
And waited in his train.

They saw his heart, transfixed with wounds,
With love and grief run o'er;
They saw him break the bars of death
Which none e'er brake before.

They brought his chariot from above
  To bear him to his throne,
Clapped their triumphant wings, and cried,
  "The glorious work is done!"

Guardian Angels.

LEIGH RICHMOND.

Hark! how the angels, as they fly,
Sing through the regions of the sky,
Bearing an infant in their arms,
Securely freed from sin's alarms.

"Welcome, dear babe, to Jesus' breast,
Forever there in joy to rest;
Welcome to Jesus' courts above,
To sing thy great Redeemer's love.

"We left the heavens and flew to earth
To watch thee at thy mortal birth;
Obedient to thy Saviour's will,
We stayed to love and guard thee still.

"We, thy protecting angels, came
To see thee blessed in Jesus' name;
When the baptismal seal was given,
To mark thee, child, an heir of heaven.

"When the resistless call of death
Bade thee resign thy infant breath,
When parents wept, and thou didst smile,
We were thy guardians all the while.

"Now with the lightning's speed we bear
The child committed to our care;
With anthems, such as angels sing,
We fly to bear thee to our King."

Thus, sweetly borne, he flies to rest;
We know 'tis well, nay, more, 'tis best;
When we our pilgrim's path have trod,
Oh, may we find him with our God!

IV. SAINTS GLORIFIED.

The Ransomed of the Lord.

GILES FLETCHER.

HERE may the band that now in triumph shines,
And that, before they were invested thus,
In earthly bodies carried heavenly minds,
Pitch round about, in order glorious,
Their sunny tents and houses luminous,
All their eternal day in songs employing,
Joying their end, without end of their joying,
While their Almighty Prince destruction is destroying.

Their sight drinks lovely fire in at their eyes;
Their breath sweet incense with fine breath accloys,
That on God's sweating altar burning lies;
Their hungry ears feed on the heavenly noise
That angels sing to tell their untold joys;
Their understanding, naked truth, their wills
The all and self-sufficient goodness fills,
That nothing here is wanting but the want of ills.

No sorrow now hangs clouding on their brow;
  No bloodless malady empales their face;
No age drops on their hairs his silver snow;
  No nakedness their bodies doth embase;
  No poverty themselves and theirs disgrace;
No fear of death the joy of life devours;
No unchaste sleep their precious time deflowers;
No loss, no grief, no change, wait on their winged
    hours.

But now their naked bodies scorn the cold,
  And from their eyes joy looks and laughs at pain;
The infant wonders how he came so old,
  The old man how he came so young again;
  Still resting, though from sleep they still refrain;
Where all are rich, and yet no gold they owe;
And all are kings, and yet no subjects know;
All full, and yet no time they do on food bestow.

About the holy city rolls a flood
  Of molten crystal, like a sea of glass,
On which weak stream a strong foundation stood;
  Of living diamonds the building was,
  That all things else, besides itself, did pass;
Her streets, instead of stones, the stars did pave,
And little pearls for dust it seemed to have,
On which soft-streaming manna like pure snow did
    wave.

It is no flaming lustre, made of light,
  No sweet consent, or well-tuned harmony,
Ambrosia, for to feast the appetite,
  Or flowery odor mixed with spicery,
  No soft embrace, or pleasure bodily;
And yet it is a kind of inward feast,
A harmony that sounds within the breast,
An odor, light, embrace, in which the soul doth rest.

A heavenly feast no hunger can consume,
  A light unseen, yet shines in every place,
A sound no time can steal, a sweet perfume
  No winds can scatter, an entire embrace
  That no satiety can e'er unlace;
Ingraced into so high a favor there,
The saints with their beau-peers whole worlds outwear,
And things unseen do see, and things unheard do hear.

Ye blessed souls, grown richer by your spoil,
  Whose loss, though great, is cause of greater gains;
Here may your wearied spirits rest from toil,
  Spending your endless evening that remains
  Among those white flocks and celestial trains
That feed upon their Shepherd's eyes, and frame
That heavenly music of so wondrous fame,
Psalming aloud the holy honors of his name.

The Cloud of Witnesses.

CHARLES WESLEY.

Ye happy souls, no longer tossed
  Like us on life's tempestuous sea,
Who cannot now be shipwrecked, lost,
  Safe landed in eternity,
Are mortals banished from your mind?
Or think ye of your friends behind?

'Tis Jesus bids us keep in view
  Your active faith and patient hope;
As ye your Lord, we follow you,
  And wait for him to take us up,
Our closest fellowship t' improve,
Our fellowship with saints above.

Till then we hold your memory dear,
  Which now relieves our drooping heart;
Like us ye mourned and suffered here;
  Like us ye languished to depart,
And labored on with painful strife,
And dragged the heavy load of life.

But oh! your evil day is past;
  Accomplished is your warfare here;
And more than conquerors at last,
  Our sad, desponding hearts ye cheer;

Ye bid us still your steps pursue,
And we shall more than conquer too.

Encompassed with so great a cloud
  Of witnesses, who speak, though dead,
We cast aside our every load,
  And follow where our Lord hath led;
With patience run the appointed race,
And die to see his glorious face.

The Emancipated.

FROM THE GERMAN OF DACH, BY LONGFELLOW.

Oh how blest are ye whose toils are ended,
Who through death have unto God ascended!
    Ye have arisen
From the cares which keep us still in prison.

We are still as in a dungeon living,
Still oppressed with sorrow and misgiving;
    Our undertakings
Are but toils, and troubles, and heart-breakings.

Ye meanwhile are in your chambers sleeping,
Quiet, and set free from all our weeping;
    No cross nor trial
Hinders your enjoyments with denial.

Christ has wiped away your tears forever;
Ye have that for which we still endeavor;
To you are chanted
Songs which no mortal ear ever haunted.

Ah! who would not, then, depart with gladness,
To inherit heaven for earthly sadness?
Who here would languish
Longer in bewailing and in anguish?

Come, O Christ, and loose the chains that bind us;
Lead us forth, and cast this world behind us;
With thee, the Anointed,
Finds the soul its joy and rest appointed.

The Celestial Army.

THOMAS B. READ.

I STOOD by the open casement
And looked upon the night,
And saw the westward going stars
Pass slowly out of sight.

Slowly the bright procession
Went down the gleaming arch,
And my soul discerned the music
Of their long, triumphal march;

Till the great celestial army,
  Stretching far beyond the poles,
Became the eternal symbol
  Of the mighty march of souls.

Onward, forever onward,
  Red Mars led down his clan;
And the moon, like a mailed maiden
  Was riding in the van.

And some were bright in beauty,
  And some were faint and small;
But these might be in their greatest height
  The noblest of them all.

Downward, forever downward,
  Behind Earth's dusky shore,
They passed into the unknown night, —
  They passed, and were no more.

No more? Oh, say not so!
  And downward is not just;
For the sight is weak and the sense is dim
  That looks through heated dust.

The stars and the mailed moon,
  Though they seem to fall and die,
Still sweep with their embattled lines
  An endless reach of sky.

And though the hills of death
  May hide the bright array,
The marshalled brotherhood of souls
  Still keeps its upward way.

Upward, forever upward,
  I see their march sublime,
And hear the glorious music
  Of the conquerors of Time.

And long let me remember
  That the palest, faintest one,
May to diviner vision be
  A bright and blessed sun.

Palm-Bearers.

J. MONTGOMERY.

PALMS of glory, raiment bright,
  Crowns that never fade away,
Gird and deck the saints in light;
  Priests, and kings, and conquerors they.

Yet the conquerors bring their palms
  To the Lamb amidst the throne,
And proclaim, in joyful psalms,
  Victory through His cross alone.

Kings for harps their crowns resign,
 Crying, as they strike the chords,
"Take the kingdom, it is thine,
 King of kings, and Lord of lords!"

Round the altar priests confess,
 If their robes are white as snow,
'Twas the Saviour's righteousness,
 And his blood, that made them so.

Who were these? On earth they dwelt,
 Sinners once of Adam's race;
Guilt, and fear, and suffering felt,
 But were saved by sovereign grace.

They were mortal, too, like us;
 Ah! when we like them must die,
May our souls, translated thus,
 Triumph, reign, and shine on high!

What are Those?

FROM THE GERMAN OF SCHENK, BY MISS WINKWORTH.

WHO are those before God's throne,
 What the crowned host I see?
As the sky, with stars thick-strown,
 Is their shining company;
Hallelujahs, hark, they sing;
Solemn praise to God they bring.

WHO ARE IN HEAVEN?

Who are those that in their hands
  Bear aloft the conqueror's palm,
As one o'er his foeman stands,
  Fallen beneath his mighty arm?
What the war and what the strife?
Whence came such victorious life?

Who are those arrayed in light,
  Clothed in righteousness divine,
Wearing robes most pure and white,
  That unstained shall ever shine,
That can never more decay?
Whence came all this bright array?

They are those who, strong in faith,
  Battled for the mighty God;
Conquerors o'er the world and death,
  Following not sin's crowded road;
Through the Lamb who once was slain,
Did they such high victory gain.

They are those who much have borne,
  Trial, sorrow, pain, and care,
Who have wrestled night and morn
  With the mighty God in prayer;
Now their strife hath found its close;
God hath turned away their woes.

They are branches of that Stem
 Who hath our salvation been;
In the blood He shed for them
 Have they made their raiment clean;
Hence they wear such radiant dress,
Clad in spotless holiness.

They are those who hourly here
 Served as priests before their Lord,
Offering up, with gladsome cheer,
 Soul and body at his word:
Now, within the holy place,
They behold him face to face.

As the harts at noonday pant
 For the river fresh and clear,
Did their souls oft long and faint
 For the living Fountain here;
Now their thirst is quenched; they dwell
With the Lord they loved so well.

Thitherwards I stretch my hands;
 O Lord Jesus, day by day,
In thy house in these strange lands,
 Compassed round with foes, I pray,
Let me sink not in the war;
Drive for me my foes afar.

Cast my lot in earth and heaven
  With thy saints, made like to thee;
Let my bonds be also riven;
  Make thy child, who loves thee, free;
Near the throne where thou dost shine,
May a place at last be mine.

Ah! that bliss can ne'er be told,
  When, with all that army bright,
Thee, my Sun, I shall behold,
  Shining, star-like, with thy light!
Amen! thanks be brought to thee,
Praise through all eternity!

The First Martyr.

TEN thousand times ten thousand sung
  Loud anthems round the throne,
When, lo! one solitary tongue
  Began a song unknown,—
A song unknown to angel ears,
A song that told of banished fears,
Of pardoned sins and dried-up tears.

Not one of all the heavenly host
  Could these high notes attain;
But spirits from a distant coast
  United in the strain,

Till he who first began the song,
To sing alone not suffered long,
Was mingled with a countless throng.

And still, as hours are fleeting by,
  The angels ever bear
Some newly-ransomed soul on high,
  To join the chorus there;
And so the song will louder grow,
Till all, redeemed by Christ below,
To that fair world of rapture go.

Oh give me, Lord, my golden harp,
  And tune my broken voice,
That I may sing of troubles sharp
  Exchanged for endless joys;
The song that ne'er was heard before,
A sinner reached the heavenly shore,
But now shall sound for evermore.

Champions of God.

H. H. MILMAN.

Sing to the Lord! let harp, and lute, and voice,
Up to the expanding gates of heaven rejoice,
  While the bright martyrs to their rest are borne;

Sing to the Lord! their blood-stained course is run,
And every head its diadem hath won,
Rich as the purple of the summer morn;
Sing the triumphant champions of their God,
While burn their mounting feet along their skyward road.

Sing to the Lord! for in her beauty's prime
Snatched from this wintry earth's ungenial clime,
In the eternal spring of Paradise to bloom;
For her the world displayed its brightest treasure,
And the airs panted with the songs of pleasure;
Before earth's throne she chose the lowly tomb,
The vale of tears with willing footsteps trod,
Bearing her cross with thee, incarnate Son of God!

Sing to the Lord! it is not shed in vain,—
The blood of martyrs; from its refreshing rain
High springs the church, like some fount-shadowing palm;
The nations crowd beneath its branching shade;
Of its green leaves are kingly diadems made,
And wrapt within its deep embosoming calm,
Earth sinks to slumber like the breezeless deep,
And war's tempestuous vultures fold their wings and sleep.

Sing to the Lord! when time itself shall cease,
And final ruin's desolating peace

Enwrap this wild and restless world of man,
When the Judge rides upon the enthroning wind,
And o'er all generations of mankind
Eternal Justice waves its winnowing fan,
To vast infinity's remotest space,
While ages run their everlasting race,
Shall all the beatific hosts prolong,
Wide as the glory of the Lamb, the Lamb's triumphant
song!

V. OUR SAINTED FRIENDS.

Our Early Friends.

HENRY ALFORD.

ONE, and another, pass they and are gone,
Our early friends. Like minute-bells of heaven,
Across our path in fitful wailings driven,
Hear we death's tidings ever and anon.
A little longer, and we stand alone;
A few more strokes of the Almighty rod,
And the dread presence of the voice of God
About our footsteps shall be heard and known.
Toil on, toil on, thou weary, weary arm;
Hope ever onward, heavy-laden heart;
Let the false charmer ne'er so wisely charm;
Listen we not, but ply our task apart,
Cheering each hour of work with thoughts of rest,
And with their love who labored and are blest.

Our Christian Brother.

CHARLES WESLEY.

WEEP not for a brother deceased;
  Our loss is his infinite gain;
A soul out of prison released,
  And freed from its bodily chain;
With songs let us follow his flight,
  And mount with his spirit above,
Escaped to the mansions of light,
  And lodged in the Eden of love.

Our brother the haven hath gained,
  Out-flying the tempest and wind;
His rest he hath sooner obtained,
  And left his companions behind,
Still tossed on a sea of distress,
  Hard toiling to make the blest shore,
Where all is assurance and peace,
  And sorrow and sin are no more.

There all the ship's company meet
  Who sailed with the Saviour beneath;
With shouting each other they greet,
  And triumph o'er sorrow and death;
The voyage of life's at an end;
  The mortal affliction is past;
The age that in heaven they spend,
  Forever and ever shall last.

Our Kindred.

J. MONTGOMERY.

THE broken ties of happier days,
  How often do they seem
To come before our mental gaze,
  Like a remembered dream!
Around us each dissevered chain
  In sparkling ruin lies,
And earthly hand can ne'er again
  Unite those broken ties.

The parents of our youthful home,
  The kindred that we loved,
Far from our arms perchance may roam,
  To desert seas removed;
Or we have watched their parting breath,
  And closed their weary eyes,
And sighed to think how sadly death
  Can sever human ties.

The friends, the loved ones of our youth,
  They, too, are gone or changed;
Or, worse than all, their love and truth
  Are darkened or estranged;
They meet us in the glittering throng
  With cold, averted eyes,
And wonder that we weep their wrong,
  And mourn our broken ties.

Oh who, in such a world as this,
Could bear their lot of pain,
Did not one radiant hope of bliss
Unclouded yet remain?
That hope the sovereign Lord has given
Who reigns above the skies,
Hope that unites our souls to heaven
By faith's enduring ties.

Each care, each ill of mortal birth,
Is sent in pitying love,
To lift the lingering heart from earth,
And speed its flight above;
And every pang that wrings the breast,
And every joy that dies,
Tells us to seek a purer rest,
And trust to holier ties.

Our Friend.

ANDREWS NORTON.

He has gone to his God, he has gone to his home,
No more amid peril and error to roam;
His eyes are no longer dim;
His feet will no more falter;
No grief can follow him;
No pang his cheek can alter.

There are paleness, and weeping, and sighs below,
For our faith is faint, and our tears will flow;
But the harps of heaven are ringing,
Glad angels come to greet him,
And hymns of joy are singing,
While old friends press to meet him.

O honored, beloved, to earth unconfined,
Thou hast soared on high, thou hast left us behind;
But our parting is not forever;
We will follow thee by heaven's light,
Where the grave cannot dissever
The souls whom God will unite.

Your Friend Rejoicing.

DR. HUIE.

Oh think that, while you're weeping here,
His hand a golden harp is stringing;
And, with a voice serene and clear,
His ransomed soul, without a tear,
His Saviour's praise is singing!

And think that all his pains are fled,
His toils and sorrows closed forever,
While He, whose blood for man was shed,
Has placed upon his servant's head
A crown that fadeth never.

And think that, in that awful day,
  When darkness sun and moon is shading,
The form that midst its kindred clay
Your trembling hands prepare to lay,
  Shall rise to life unfading!

Then weep no more for him who's gone
  Where sin and suffering ne'er shall enter;
But on that great High Priest alone,
Who can for guilt like ours atone,
  Your own affections centre.

For thus, while round your lowly bier
  Surviving friends are sadly bending,
Your souls, like his, to Jesus dear,
Shall wing their flight to yonder sphere,
  Faith lightest pinions lending.

And thus, when to the silent tomb
  Your lifeless dust like his is given,
Like faith shall whisper, midst the gloom,
That yet again, in youthful bloom,
  That dust shall smile in heaven.

The Matron.

MISS C. E. ROBERTS.

"Is this her home?"
I ask, in earnest tone.
All that make home are here, —
Husband, and children dear,
And kindred hearts, which ever seem to be
Full of kind love and gentle sympathy;
But desolate they stand,
That little household band;
Most mournful is the crying
I hear, in sad replying
Unto my earnest tone,
"Is this her home?"

"Is this her home?"
I ask, in earnest tone.
The new-laid turf is green,
And the sweet flowers, I ween,
Will love to come and deck the lowly bed,
Where in calm slumbers rests that youthful head.
The wild bird's song is here,
The sunshine bright and clear;
O peace! she's sweetly sleeping,
While we the watch are keeping;
Why answer still with weeping
Unto my earnest tone,
"Is this her home?"

"Is this her home?"
I ask, in solemn tone.
Behold, the Lord is here;
The Lamb of God is near,
To lead her into pastures ever fair,
And point her to the living waters there;
See! robed in light she stands
Amid the angel bands;
Her hand a harp is stringing;
Its notes through heaven are ringing;
Oh, list! the song she's singing,
Most joyful is the tone,
"Heaven is my home."

Where is my Friend?

MRS. ANNA L. BARBAULD.

PURE spirit! Oh where art thou now?
Oh whisper to my soul!
Oh let some soothing thought of thee
This bitter grief control!

'Tis not for thee the tears I shed;
Thy sufferings now are o'er;
The sea is calm, the tempest past,
On that eternal shore.

No more the storms that wreck thy peace
  Shall tear that gentle breast,
Nor summer's rage, nor winter's cold,
  Thy poor, poor frame molest.

Thy peace is sealed, thy rest is sure;
  My sorrows are to come;
Awhile I weep and linger here,
  Then follow to the tomb.

And is the awful veil withdrawn
  That shrouds from mortal eyes,
In deep, impenetrable gloom,
  The secrets of the skies?

Oh, in some dream of visioned bliss,
  Some trance of rapture, show
Where, on the bosom of thy God,
  Thou rest'st from human woe!

Thence may thy pure devotion's flame
  On me, on me descend;
To me thy strong, aspiring hopes,
  Thy faith, thy fervors, lend.

Let these my lonely path illume,
  And teach my wakened mind
To welcome all that's left of good,
  To all that's lost resigned.

Farewell! with honor, peace, and love,
Be thy dear memory blest!
Thou hast no tears for me to shed,
When I, too, am at rest.

Who Believed and Loved.

JOHN MILTON.

When Faith and Love, which parted from thee never,
Had ripened thy just soul to dwell with God,
Meekly thou didst resign this earthly load
Of death, called life, which us from life doth sever.
Thy works, and alms, and all thy good endeavor,
Staid not behind, nor in the grave were trod;
But, as Faith pointed with her golden rod,
Followed thee up to joy and bliss forever.
Love led them on, and Faith, who knew them best,
Thy handmaids, clad them o'er with purple beams
And azure wings, that up they flew so drest,
And spake the truth of thee on glorious themes
Before the Judge, who henceforth bade thee rest,
And drink thy fill of pure immortal streams.

She is in Heaven.

CHARLOTTE ELLIOTT.

SHE is in heaven! That thought alone
  Should chase the grief which clouds thy brow;
'Twas said, from her Redeemer's throne,
  "Into my joy now enter thou!"

She is in heaven. How sweet the phrase!
  Yet its high import who can tell?
Here like a glimmering beam it plays,
  Of light, of joy ineffable.

She is in heaven, lest earthly love,
  So sweet, so strong as hers and thine,
To both might too attractive prove,
  Stealing the place of love divine.

She is in heaven, to form a link
  Between thy heart and worlds unseen,
That there, where nature's powers must sink,
  Faith's holier virtue may be seen.

She is in heaven, that thou mayst waste
  No thought, no care, on earthly things,
But travel with an angel's haste,
  And soar as on an angel's wings.

She is in heaven, that thou, like her,
  Mayst shine with pure and steadfast light;
Attract their eye whose footsteps err,
  And guide their wandering feet aright.

She is in heaven, but still, unseen,
  With hers thy notes of praise may blend;
On the same Rock thy soul may lean,
  To the same centre hourly tend.

She is in heaven, that thou mayst prove
  How blest the Christian's darkest lot;
Earth's joys may fail, earth's props remove,
  But God, thy portion, changes not.

She is in heaven. When thou art faint,
  And wouldst thy weary race were run,
Think that the voice of that loved saint
  Whispers, "The prize will soon be won!"

She is in heaven, — has crossed ere noon
  The stream which bounds th' eternal land, —
And wilt thou not rejoin her soon?
  Yes, though till eve thou waiting stand.

My Husband.

SAY, how can I with lightsome feet
  Life's rugged pathway tread,
Since he who once did cheer me on
  Lies silent now and dead,
No more with soothing words to cheer,
And soon disperse my rising fear?

How can I to the festive board
  A willing guest repair,
Since he who was my earthly all
  Will not conduct me there?
'Tis vain for me to spread the feast,
Since he I love is not a guest.

And when around the quiet hearth
  My children fondly meet,
What anguish fills my inmost soul
  To see that vacant seat,
Where the loved father used to smile,
And our obtruding cares beguile.

But why indulge these notes of grief?
  Why should I thus complain?
What now to me is loss severe
  Is his eternal gain.
I bow submissive to the rod;
It raised a saint to dwell with God.

A few more suns may run their course,
While I in sadness weep,
Then by his side in sweet repose
I shall securely sleep;
Then shall my soul with rapture soar
Where saints shall meet to part no more!

Not Lost.

"The loved and lost!" why do we call them lost
Because we miss them from our onward road?
God's unseen angel o'er our pathway crossed,
Looked on us all, and loving them the most,
Straightway relieved them from life's weary load.

They are not lost; they are within the door
That shuts out loss, and every hurtful thing,
With angels bright, and loved ones gone before,
In their Redeemer's presence evermore,
And God himself their Lord, and Judge, and King.

And this we call a loss; O selfish sorrow
Of selfish hearts! O we of little faith!
Let us look round, some argument to borrow,
Why we in patience should await the morrow
That surely must succeed this night of death.

Ay, look upon this dreary desert path,
  The thorns and thistles wheresoe'er we turn;
What trials and what tears, what wrongs and wrath,
What struggles and what strife, the journey hath!
  They have escaped from these, and, lo! we mourn.

Ask the poor sailor, when the wreck is done,
  Who with his treasures strove the shore to reach,
While with the raging waves he battled on,
Was it not joy, where every joy seemed gone,
  To see his loved ones landed on the beach?

A poor wayfarer, leading by the hand
  A little child, hath halted by the well
To wash from off her feet the clinging sand,
And tell the tired boy of that bright land
  Where, this long journey past, they longed to dwell;

When, lo! the Lord, who many mansions had,
  Drew near and looked upon the suffering twain,
Then, pitying, spake, "Give me the little lad;"
In strength renewed, and glorious beauty clad,
  I'll bring him with me when I come again."

Did she make answer selfishly and wrong, —
  "Nay, but the woes I feel he too must share!"
Oh, rather, bursting into grateful song,
She went her way rejoicing, and made strong
  To struggle on, since he was freed from care.

We will do likewise; death hath made no breach
  In love and sympathy, in hope and trust;
No outward sign or sound our ears can reach,
But there's an inward, spiritual speech,
  That greets us still, though mortal tongues be dust.

It bids us do the work that they laid down,
  Take up the song where they broke off the strain,
So journeying till we reach the heavenly town
Where are laid up our treasures and our crown,
  And our lost loved ones will be found again.

VI. REDEEMED CHILDREN.

The One Wanted.

GOD looked among his cherub band,
And one was wanting there
To swell along the holy land
The hymns of praise and prayer.

One little soul which long had been
Half way 'tween earth and sky,
Untempted in a world of sin,
He watched with loving eye.

It was too promising a flower
To bloom upon this earth,
And God did give it angel power,
And bright celestial birth.

The world was all too bleak and cold
To yield it quiet rest;
God brought it to his shepherd-fold,
And laid it on his breast.

There, mother, in thy Saviour's arms,
Forever undefiled,
Amid the little cherub band,
Is thy beloved child.

The Lambs of Christ.

THEY were gathered early, earth's young and fair;
Time cannot touch them, nor woe, nor care;
Safe in the harbor of endless rest,
The babes are cradled on Jesus' breast.

There are eyes of sapphire, and locks of gold,
And roseate hues, in that little fold;
Music untaught, like the wild bird's song,
In gushes burst from the cherub throng.

From silken couches, and beds of down,
Through the dusky ways of the crowded town,
By hall, and village, and moorland bleak,
Have the angels travelled those buds to seek.

And some who were born to an earthly crown,
When the angels whispered, they laid it down;
'Twas a weary weight for those tiny heads,
So they died uncrowned in their little beds.

There are those who were born in grief and shame,
Without mother's love, or a father's name;
O'er their lamp of life the chill night-wind swept;
They were laid in the earth unowned, unwept.

There are some for whom gray heads toiled and planned,
And they hoarded gold, and they purchased land;
The innocent heirs of a sordid care,
They were snatched from the teeth of the gilded snare.

There are some who were taken, we know not why,
By the love that walketh in mystery,
The mercy that moves behind sunless clouds;
For earth's saints wept o'er their early shrouds.

There are those o'er whom solemn tears were shed
By parents who struggled for daily bread,
Who mourned o'er the soul they brought to strife;
But the angels gave it the bread of life.

They are one in heaven,—the wept and dear,
The foundling who perished without a tear,
Of lands and titles earth's infant heir,
And the blighted offspring of want and care.

The lambs of Christ! by the founts and rills,
O'er the heights of the everlasting hills,
They follow with joy the Bridegroom's train:
If ye love, can ye wish them back again?

Where are they Now?

WHERE are they now who used at morn to gambol,
Like bounding roebucks, in our sunny path?
Where are they now who shared our evening ramble,
And made the green wood vocal with their laugh?
Where are they now, from earth's glad pathway riven?
We trust, in heaven.

Where are they now? The early birds are singing
Their joyful melodies to earth and air,
While all around the song of hope is ringing;
Why come they not with us the scene to share?
No; higher joys than ours to them are given,
We trust, in heaven.

Where are they now? The spring's young charms are breaking,
To deck fair nature with their budding bloom;
All things from winter's cold embrace are waking—
All save the tenants of the dreary tomb;
Their spring shall dawn, and death's dark bonds be riven,
We trust, in heaven.

Sweet Babes.

CHARLOTTE ELLIOTT.

Oh could I pierce that deep abyss
Which parts the unseen world from this,
I would behold your seats in bliss,
Sweet babes!

Would view your souls without a stain,
In God's own image bright again,
And feel that death for you was gain,
Sweet babes!

And I would hear that matchless song
Swelled by the bright celestial throng,
And catch your notes the choir among,
Sweet babes!

Thrice happy travellers! how soon
Your task is o'er, your work is done;
How short a race your prize has won,
Sweet babes!

No toil nor care ye need bestow
To make the flowers of virtue blow;
Spontaneous in that clime they grow,
Sweet babes!

There, sown in a congenial bed,
Each heavenly blossom rears its head,
There blooms, and there is perfected,
Sweet babes!

And can we mourn that God, in love,
Saw fit so early to remove
Your spirits to his courts above,
Sweet babes?

In this dark world, with dangers fraught,
What snares your footsteps might have caught,
What woe and ruin sin have wrought,
Sweet babes!

There was a heavenly Friend who knew
What perils would your path bestrew,
And in his arms he sheltered you,
Sweet babes!

From earth's polluted region far,
He bade you breathe a purer air;
How pure, when God himself is there,
Sweet babes!

Could those who now their couch bedew
With bitter tears your glory view,
Ne'er would they weep again for you,
Sweet babes!

But feel love's earthly tie was riven
Only to be forever given
A golden link 'twixt earth and heaven,
Sweet babes!

My Child Safe.

MRS. C. A. SOUTHEY.

God took thee in his mercy,
A lamb untasked, untried;
He fought the fight for thee,
He won the victory,
And thou art sanctified.

I look around and see
The evil ways of men,
And, oh! beloved child,
I'm more than reconciled
To thy departure then.

The little arms that clasped me,
The innocent life that pressed,
Would they have been as pure
Till now as when of yore
I lulled thee on my breast?

Now like a dew-drop shrined
Within a crystal stone,
Thou'rt safe in heaven, my dove,
Safe with the Source of love,
The Everlasting One.

And when the hour arrives
From flesh that sets me free,
Thy spirit may await
The first at heaven's gate
To meet and welcome me.

My Child Promoted.

THOMAS WARD.

Thou bright and starlike spirit,
That, in my visions wild,
I see 'mid heaven's seraphic host,
Oh, canst thou be my child?

My grief is quenched in wonder,
And pride arrests my sighs;
A branch from this unworthy stock
Now blossoms in the skies.

Our hopes of thee were lofty;
But have we cause to grieve?
Oh, could our fondest, proudest wish
A nobler fate conceive?—

A little weeper tearless,
The sinner snatched from sin,
The babe to more than manhood grown
Ere childhood did begin?

And I, thy earthly teacher,
Would blush thy powers to see;
Thou art to me a parent now,
And I a child to thee.

What bliss is born of sorrow!
'Tis never sent in vain;
The heavenly Surgeon maims to save;
He gives no useless pain.

Our God, to call us homeward,
His only Son sent down,
And now, still more to tempt our hearts,
Has taken up our own.

My Son in Glory.

FROM THE SYRIAC OF EPHRAEM SYRUS.

CHILD, by God's sweet mercy given
  To thy mother and to me,
Entering this world of sorrows,
  By his grace, so fair to see,
Fair as some sweet flower in summer,
  Till death's hand on thee was laid,
Scorched the beauty from my flower,
  Made the tender petals fade;
Yet I dare not weep nor murmur,
  For I know the King of kings
Leads thee to his marriage-chamber,
  To the glorious bridal brings.

Nature fain would have me weeping;
  Love asserts her mournful right;
But I answer, they have brought thee
  To the happy world of light;
And I fear that my lamentings,
  As I speak thy cherished name,
Desecrate the royal dwelling;—
  Fear to meet deserved blame,
If I press, with tears of anguish,
  Into the abode of joy;
Therefore will I, meekly bowing,
  Offer thee to God, my boy.

Yet thy voice, thy childish singing,
  Soundeth ever in my ears,
And I listen, and remember,
  Till my eyes will gather tears,
Thinking of thy pretty prattlings,
  And thy childish words of love;
But when I begin to murmur,
  Then my spirit looks above,
Listens to the songs of spirits,
  Listens, longing, wondering,
To the ceaseless glad hosannas
  Angels at thy bridal sing.

My Own Dear Son.

FROM THE GERMAN OF PAUL GERHARD, BY MISS WINKWORTH.

THOU 'rt mine, yes, still thou art mine own;
  Who tells me thou art lost?
But yet thou art not mine alone;
  I own that He who crossed
My hopes hath greater right in thee;
Yea, though he ask and take from me
Thee, O my son, my heart's delight,
My wish, my thought, by day and night.

Ah, might I wish, ah, might I choose,
  Then thou, my star, shouldst live,
And gladly for thy sake I'd lose
  All else that life can give;
Oh fain I'd say, Abide with me,
The sunshine of my house to be;
No other joy but this I crave,
To love thee, darling, to my grave.

Thus saith my heart, and means it well;
  God meaneth better still;
My love is more than words can tell,
  His love is greater still;
I am a father, he the Head
And Crown of fathers, whence is shed
The life and love from which have sprung
All blessed ties in old and young.

I long for thee, my son, my own,
  And He who once hath given
Will have thee now beside his throne,
  To live with him in heaven.
I cry, Alas, my light, my child!
But God hath welcome on him smiled,
And said, "My child, I keep thee near,
For there is nought but gladness here."

Oh blessed word, oh deep decree,
More holy than we think!
With God no grief or woe can be;
No bitter cup to drink,
No sickening hopes, no want or care,
No hurt, can ever reach him there;
Yes, in that Father's sheltered home
I know that sorrow cannot come.

We pass our nights in wakeful thought
For our dear children's sake;
All day our anxious toil hath sought
How best for them to make
A future safe from care or need;
Yet seldom do our schemes succeed;
How seldom does their future prove
What we had planned for those we love.

How many a child of promise fair
Ere now hath gone astray,
By ill example taught to dare
Forsake Christ's holy way;
Oh fearful the reward is then,
The wrath of God, the scorn of men!
The bitterest tears that e'er are shed
Are his who mourns a child misled.

But now I need not fear for thee;
  Where thou art all is well;
For thou thy Father's face dost see,
  With Jesus thou dost dwell!
Yes, cloudless joys around him shine;
His heart shall never ache like mine;
He sees the radiant armies glow
That keep and guide us here below.

He hears their singing evermore;
  His little voice, too, sings;
He drinks of wisdom's deepest lore;
  He speaks of secret things
That we can never see or know,
Howe'er we seek or strive, below,
While yet amid the mists we stand
That veil this dark and tearful land.

Oh that I could but watch afar,
  And hearken but a while
To that sweet song that hath no jar,
  And see his heavenly smile
As he doth praise the holy God
Who made him pure for that abode!
In tears of joy full well I know
This burdened heart would overflow;

And I should say, Stay here, my son,
  My wild laments are o'er;
Oh well for thee that thou hast won;
  I call thee back no more;
But come, thou fiery chariot, come,
And bear me swiftly to that home
Where he with many a loved one dwells,
And evermore of gladness tells.

Then be it as my Father wills;
  I will not weep for thee;
Thou livest; joy thy spirit fills;
  Pure sunshine thou dost see,
The sunshine of eternal rest.
Abide, my child, where thou art blest;
I with our friends will onward fare,
And, when God wills, shall find thee there.

Angel Charlie.

EMILY C. JUDSON.

He came, a beauteous vision,
  Then vanished from my sight,
His wing one moment cleaving
  The blackness of my night;

My glad ear caught its rustle,
Then, sweeping by, he stole
The dew-drop that his coming
Had cherished in my soul.

Oh, he had been my solace
When grief my spirit swayed,
And on his fragile being
Had tender hopes been stayed;
Where thought, where feeling lingered,
His form was sure to glide,
And in the lone night watches
'Twas ever by my side.

He came; but as the blossom
Its petals closes up,
And hides them from the tempest
Within its shattering cup,
So he his spirit gathered
Back to his frightened breast,
And passed from earth's grim threshold,
To be the Saviour's guest.

My boy, ah me! the sweetness,
The anguish of that word!
My boy, when in strange night-dreams
My slumbering soul is stirred,

When music floats around me,
  When soft lips touch my brow,
And whisper gentle greetings,
  Oh, tell me, is it thou?

I know, by one sweet token,
  My Charlie is not dead;
One golden clue he left me,
  As on his track he sped:
Were he some gem or blossom
  But fashioned for to-day,
My love would slowly perish
  With his dissolving clay.

Oh, by this deathless yearning,
  Which is not idly given,
By the delicious nearness
  My spirit feels to heaven,
By dreams that throng my night-sleep,
  By visions of the day,
By whispers when I'm erring,
  By promptings when I pray,—

I know this life so cherished,
  Which sprang beneath my heart,
Which formed of my own being
  So beautiful a part,

This precious, winsome creature,
  My unfledged, voiceless dove,
Lifts now a seraph's pinion,
  And warbles lays of love.

Oh, I would not recall thee,
  My glorious angel-boy;
Thou needest not my bosom,
  Rare bird of light and joy;
Here dash I down the tear-drops,
  Still gathering in my eyes,
Blest — oh, how blest! — in adding
  A seraph to the skies!

Our Infant Daughter.

J. W. CUNNINGHAM.

Sweet babe, she glanced into our world to see
A sample of our misery,
Then turned away her languid eye
To drop a tear or two, and die.
Sweet babe, she tasted of life's bitter cup,
Refused to drink the potion up;
But turned her little head aside,
Disgusted with the taste, and died.

Sweet babe, she listened for a while to hear
Our mortal griefs, then turned her ear
To angels' harps and songs, and cried
To join their notes celestial, sighed, and died.

Sweet babe no more, but seraph now,
Before the throne behold her bow;
To heavenly joys her spirit flies,
Blest in the triumph of the skies,
Adores the grace that brought her there
Without a wish, without a care,
That washed her soul in Calvary's stream,
That shortened life's distressing dream;
Short pain, short grief, dear babe, was thine,
Now joys eternal and divine.

Yes, thou art fled, and saints a welcome sing;
Thine infant spirit soars on angel's wing;
Our dark affection should have hoped thy stay;
The voice of God has called his child away,
Like Samuel, early in the temple found;
Sweet rose of Sharon, plant of holy ground,
Oh, more than Samuel blest, to thee 'tis given
The God he served on earth to serve in heaven!

A Lamb Folded.

FROM THE GERMAN OF W. MEINHOLD, BY MISS WINKWORTH.

Gentle Shepherd, thou hast stilled
  Now thy little lamb's long weeping;
Ah! how peaceful, pale, and mild,
  In its narrow bed 'tis sleeping;
And no sigh of anguish sore
Heaves that little bosom more.

In this world of care and pain,
  Lord, thou wouldst no longer leave it;
To the sunny heavenly plain
  Dost thou now with joy receive it;
Clothed in robes of spotless white,
Now it dwells with thee in light.

Ah, Lord Jesus, grant that we
  Where it lives may soon be living,
And the lovely pastures see
  That its heavenly food are giving;
Then the gain of death we prove,
Though thou take what most we love.

IV.

What are they Doing in Heaven?

WHAT ARE THEY DOING IN HEAVEN?

Adoring the Saviour.

ISAAC WATTS.

DESCEND from heaven, immortal Dove,
Stoop down and take us on thy wings,
And mount and bear us far above
The reach of these inferior things;

Beyond, beyond this lower sky,
Up where eternal ages roll,
Where solid pleasures never die,
And fruits immortal feast the soul.

Oh for a sight, a pleasing sight,
Of our almighty Father's throne!
There sits our Saviour crowned with light,
Clothed in a body like our own.

Adoring saints around him stand,
And thrones and powers before him fall;
The God shines gracious through the man,
And sheds sweet glories on them all.

Oh what amazing joys they feel,
While to their golden harps they sing,
And sit on every heavenly hill,
And spread the triumphs of their King!

When shall the day, dear Lord, appear
That I shall mount to dwell above,
And stand and bow amongst them there,
And view thy face, and sing, and love?

Harping with their Harps.

Hark! hark! the voice of ceaseless praise
Around Jehovah's throne!
Songs of celestial joy they raise
To mortal lips unknown.

Upon the sea of glass they stand,
In shining robes of light;
The harps of God are in their hand;
They rest not day or night.

Oh for an angel's perfect love,
A seraph's soaring wing,
To sing, with thousand saints above,
The triumphs of our King.

On earth our feeble voice we try,
In weakness and in shame;
We bless, we laud, we magnify,
We conquer in his name.

But, oh! with pure and sinless heart
His mercies to adore,
My God, to know thee as thou art,
Nor grieve thy Spirit more!

Oh, blessed hope! a "little while,"
And we, amidst that throng,
Shall live in our Redeemer's smile,
And swell the angels' song.

Seraphs with Elevated Strains.

ISAAC WATTS.

SERAPHS with elevated strains
Circle the throne around,
And move and charm the starry plains
With an immortal sound.

Jesus the Lord their harps employs;
Jesus, my love, they sing;
Jesus, the name of both our joys,
Sounds sweet from every string.

Hark, how beyond the narrow bounds
  Of time and space they run,
And speak, in most majestic sounds,
  The Godhead of the Son;

How on the Father's breast he lay,
  The darling of his soul,
Infinite years before the day
  Or heavens began to roll.

And now they sink the lofty tones,
  And gentler notes they play,
And bring the eternal Godhead down
  To dwell in humble clay.

Oh sacred beauties of the Man!
  The God resides within;
His flesh all pure, without a stain,
  His soul without a sin.

Then how he looked, and how he smiled;
  What wondrous things he said!
Sweet cherubs, stay, dwell here a while,
  And tell what Jesus did.

At his command the blind awake,
  And feel the gladsome rays;
He bids the dumb attempt to speak,
  They try their tongues in praise.

He shed a thousand blessings round
Where'er he turned his eye;
He spoke, and at the sovereign sound
The hellish legions fly.

Thus, while with unambitious strife
Th' ethereal minstrels rove
Through all the labors of his life
And wonders of his love,

In the full choir a broken string
Groans with a strange surprise;
The rest in silence mourn their King,
That bleeds, and loves, and dies.

Seraph and saint, with drooping wings,
Cease their harmonious breath;
No blooming trees, nor bubbling springs,
While Jesus sleeps in death.

Then all at once to living strains
They summon every chord,
Break up the tomb, and burst his chains,
And show their rising Lord.

Around the flaming army throngs
To guard him to the skies,
With loud hosannas on their tongues,
And triumph in their eyes.

In awful state the conquering God
  Ascends his shining throne,
While tuneful angels sound abroad
  The victories he has won.

Now let me rise and join their song,
  And be an angel too;
My heart, my hand, my ear, my tongue,
  Here's joyful work for you.

I would begin the music here,
  And so my soul should rise;
Oh for some heavenly notes to bear
  My spirit to the skies!

There ye that love my Saviour sit;
  There I would fain have place,
Amongst your thrones, or at your feet,
  So I might see his face.

I am confined to earth no more,
  But mount in haste above,
To bless the God that I adore,
  And sing the Man I love.

Extolling Jesus the King.

THOMAS KELLEY.

HARK! ten thousand harps and voices
  Sound the notes of praise above;
Jesus reigns, and heaven rejoices;
  Jesus reigns, the God of love;
See, he sits on yonder throne;
Jesus rules the world alone.

King of glory, reign forever,
  Thine an everlasting crown;
Nothing from thy love shall sever
  Those whom thou hast made thine own;
Happy objects of thy grace,
Destined to behold thy face.

Saviour, hasten thine appearing;
  Bring, oh bring the glorious day,
When, the awful summons hearing,
  Heaven and earth shall pass away;
Then, with golden harps, we'll sing,
"Glory, glory to our King!"

Singing "Worthy the Lamb."

J. MONTGOMERY.

Sing we the song of those who stand
  Around the eternal throne,
Of every kindred, clime, and land,
  A multitude unknown.

Life's poor distinctions vanish here;
  To-day the young, the old,
Our Saviour and his flock, appear
  One Shepherd and one fold.

Toil, trial, suffering, still await
  On earth the pilgrim throng;
Yet learn we, in our low estate,
  The church triumphant's song.

"Worthy the Lamb for sinners slain,"
  Cry the redeemed above,
"Blessing and honor to obtain,
  And everlasting love."

"Worthy the Lamb," on earth we sing,
  "Who died our souls to save;
Henceforth, O Death, where is thy sting?
  Thy victory, O Grave?"

Then hallelujah! power and praise
To God in Christ be given;
May all who now this anthem raise
Renew the strain in heaven!

Singing Alleluia.

FROM THE LATIN.

ALLELUIA! sweetest music, voice of everlasting joy!
Alleluia is the language which the heavenly hosts employ,
As they ever sing to God,
In that pure and blest abode.

Alleluia! joyful mother, true Jerusalem above!
Alleluia is the music which thy happy children love;
Exiles, tears our songs must steep;
Oft by Babel's streams we weep.

Alleluia cannot ever be our joyous psalm below;
Alleluia — sin will cross it often here with tones of woe;
Many a mournful hour we know
When our tears for sin must flow.

Therefore, 'mid our tears still praising, grant us, blessed Trinity,
Thy true paschal feast hereafter in the heavenly home to see,
Where our song shall ever be,
Alleluia unto thee!

Singing Holy, Holy, Holy.

LORD, thy glory fills the heaven;
  Earth is with its fulness stored;
Unto thee be glory given,
  Holy, holy, holy Lord!
Heaven is still with anthems ringing;
  Earth takes up the angels' cry,
Holy, holy, holy, singing,
  Lord of hosts, thou Lord most high!

Ever thus in God's high praises,
  Brethren, let our tongues unite,
While our thoughts his greatness raises,
  And our love his gifts excite.
With his seraph train before him,
  With his holy church below,
Thus unite we to adore him,
  Bid we thus our anthem flow.

Lord, thy glory fills the heaven;
  Earth is with its fulness stored;
Unto thee be glory given,
  Holy, holy, holy Lord.
Thus thy glorious name confessing,
  We adopt the angels' cry,
Holy, holy, holy, blessing
  Thee, the Lord our God most high.

Adoring the Trinity.

FROM THE LATIN OF THOMAS À KEMPIS.

HIGH the angel choirs are raising
  Heart and voice in harmony,
The Creator King still praising,
  Whom in beauty there they see.

Sweetest strains from soft harps stealing,
Trumpets notes of triumph pealing,
Radiant wings and white stoles gleaming,
Up the steps of glory streaming,
Where the heavenly bells are ringing,
Holy, holy, holy, singing,
  To the mighty Trinity;
Holy, holy, holy, crying,
For all earthly care and sighing
  In that city cease to be.

Every voice is there harmonious,
Praising God in hymns symphonious;
Love each heart with light enfolding,
As they stand in peace beholding
  There the triune Deity,
Whom adore the seraphim,
  Aye, with love eternal burning,

Venerate the cherubim,
  To their fount of honor turning,
Whilst angelic throngs adoring
  Gaze upon his majesty.

Oh how beautiful that region,
And how fair that heavenly legion,
  Where thus men and angels blend!
Glorious will that city be,
Full of deep tranquillity,
  Light and peace from end to end.
All the happy dwellers there
  Shine in robes of purity,
  Keep the law of charity,
  Bound in firmest unity;
Labor finds them not, nor care;
  Ignorance can ne'er perplex,
  Nothing tempt them, nothing vex;
  Joy and health their fadeless blessing,
  Always all good things possessing.

V.

What is the Way to Heaven?

WHAT IS THE WAY TO HEAVEN?

Know ye the Land and the Way?

FROM THE GERMAN, BY C. T. BROOKS.

KNOW ye the land? Oh! not on earth it
lies
For which the heart in hours of trouble
sighs;
Where flows no tear, no sorrow mars the
song,
The good are happy, and the weak are
strong.
Know ye the land?
The goal, the goal,
O friends, is there! Press on with heart and soul.

Know ye the way, the rough and thorny road?
The wanderer groans beneath his painful load;
He faints — he sinks; in dust he lifts his eyes;
"How long, O Lord?" the weary pilgrim sighs.
Know ye the way?
It tends, it tends
To that blest land where every torment ends.

Know ye the Friend, a man, a child of earth,
Yet more, far more than all of human birth?
That rough and thorny road his feet have trod;
Well can he guide poor pilgrims home to God.
Know ye the Friend?
His hand, his hand
Conducts us safely to our native land.

How can we know the Way?

FROM THE GERMAN OF F. SCHILLER.

From out this dim and gloomy hollow,
Where hang the cold clouds heavily,
Could I but gain the clue to follow,
How blessed would the journey be!

Aloft I see a fair dominion,
Through time and change all vernal still;
But where the power, and what the pinion,
To gain the ever-blooming hill?

Afar I hear the music ringing,
The lulling sounds of heaven's repose;
And the light gales are downward bringing
The sweets of flowers the mountain knows.

I see the fruits, all golden glowing,
  Beckon the glossy leaves between;
And o'er the blooms that there are blowing
  Nor blight nor winter's wrath hath been.

To suns that shine forever yonder,
  O'er fields that fade not, sweet to flee;
The very winds that there may wander,
  How healing must their breathing be!

Christ the Way.

THOMAS B. READ.

A weary, wandering soul am I,
  O'erburthened with an earthly weight,
A pilgrim through the world and sky,
  Toward the celestial gate.

Tell me, ye sweet and sinless flowers
  Who all night gaze upon the skies,
Have ye not in the silent hours
  Seen aught of Paradise?

Ye birds, that soar and sing, elate
  With joy, that makes your voices strong,
Have ye not at the golden gate
  Caught somewhat of your song?

Ye waters, sparkling in the morn,
  Ye seas, which glass the starry night,
Have ye not from the imperial bourn
  Caught glimpses of its light?

Ye hermit oaks and sentinel pines,
  Ye mountain forests old and gray,
In all your long and winding lines,
  Have ye not seen the way?

O moon, among thy starry bowers,
  Know'st thou the path the angels tread?
Seest thou beyond thy azure towers
  The shining gates dispread?

Ye holy spheres, that sang with earth
  When earth was still a sinless star,
Have the immortals heavenly birth
  Within your realms afar?

And thou, O sun, whose light unfurls
  Bright banners through unnumbered skies,
Seest thou among thy subject worlds
  The radiant portals rise?

All, all are mute; and still am I
  O'erburthened with an earthly weight,
A pilgrim through the world and sky,
  Towards the celestial gate.

No answer, wheresoe'er I roam,
From skies afar no guiding ray;
But hark! the voice of Christ says, "Come,
Arise, I am the way."

Christ the Way and the Life.

JAMES R. LOWELL.

I SAW a gate; a harsh voice spake and said,
"This is the gate of Life;" above was writ,
"Leave hope behind, all ye who enter it;"
Then shrank my heart within itself for dread;
But, softer than the summer rain is shed,
Words dropped upon my soul, and they did say,
"Fear nothing; faith shall save thee; watch and pray."
So, without fear, I lifted up my head,
And, lo! that writing was not; one fair word
Was carven in its stead, and it was "Love."
Then rained once more those sweet tones from above,
With healing on their wings: I humbly heard,
"I am the Life; ask, and it shall be given;
I am the Way; by me ye enter heaven."

Following Christ.

FROM THE GERMAN, BY MARY HOWITT.

THERE is a land where beauty cannot fade,
Nor sorrow dim the eye,
Where true love shall not droop nor be dismayed,
And none shall ever die.
Where is that land, oh, where?
For I would hasten there;
Tell me; I fain would go,
For I am wearied with a heavy woe;
The beautiful have left me all alone;
The true, the tender, from my path have gone;
Oh, guide me with thy hand,
If thou dost know that land,
For I am burdened with oppressive care,
And I am weak and fearful with despair!
Where is it? tell me where,
Thou, who art kind and gentle, tell me where!

Friend, thou must trust in Him who trod before
The desolate paths of life,
Must bear in meekness, as he meekly bore,
Sorrow, and pain, and strife.
Think how the Son of God
These thorny paths has trod;
Think how he longed to go,
Yet tarried out for thee the appointed woe;

Think of his weariness in places dim,
When no man comforted nor cared for him!
Think of the blood-like sweat
With which his brow was wet,
Yet how he prayed, unaided and alone,
In that great agony, "Thy will be done!"
Friend, do thou not despair,
Christ from his heaven of heavens will hear thy
prayer.

Jesus, Still Lead On.

FROM THE GERMAN OF COUNT ZINZENDORF.

JESUS, still lead on,
Till our rest be won;
And, although the way be cheerless,
We will follow, calm and fearless;
Guide us by thy hand
To our fatherland.

If the way be drear,
If the foe be near,
Let not faithless fears o'ertake us,
Let not faith and hope forsake us;
For through many a foe
To our home we go.

When we seek relief
From a long-felt grief,
When temptations come alluring,
Make us patient and enduring;
Show us that bright shore
Where we weep no more.

Jesus, still lead on,
Till our rest be won;
Heavenly Leader, still direct us,
Still support, console, protect us,
Till we safely stand
In our fatherland.

Through Trials.

FROM THE GERMAN OF KOSEGARTEN.

THROUGH night to light. And though to mortal eyes
Creation's face a pall of horror wear,
Good cheer, good cheer! The gloom of midnight flies;
Then shall a sunrise follow, mild and fair.

Through storm to calm. And though his thunder car
The rumbling tempest drive through earth and sky,
Good cheer, good cheer! The elemental war
Tells that a blessed healing hour is nigh.

Through frost to spring. And though the biting blast
  Of Eurus stiffen nature's juicy veins,
Good cheer, good cheer! When winter's wrath is past,
  Soft murmuring spring breathes sweetly o'er the plains.

Through strife to peace. And though with bristling front
  A thousand frightful depths encompass thee,
Good cheer, good cheer! Brave thou the battle's brunt,
  For the peace march and song of victory.

Through sweat to sleep. And though the sultry noon,
  With heavy, drooping wing, oppress thee now,
Good cheer, good cheer! The cool of evening soon
  Shall lull to sweet repose thy weary brow.

Through cross to crown. And though thy spirit's life
  Trials untold assail with giant strength,
Good cheer, good cheer! Soon ends the bitter strife,
  And thou shalt reign in peace with Christ at length.

Through woe to joy. And though at morn thou weep,
  And though the midnight find thee weeping still,
Good cheer, good cheer! The Shepherd loves his sheep;
  Resign thee to the watchful Father's will.

Through death to life. And through this vale of tears,
  And through this thistle-field of life, ascend
To the great supper in that world whose years
  Of bliss unfading, cloudless, know no end.

Through Perils.

Is this the way, my Father? 'Tis, my child;
Thou must pass through this tangled, dreary wild,
If thou wouldst reach the city undefiled,
Thy peaceful home above.

But enemies are round. Yes, child, I know
That where thou least expect'st thou'lt find a foe;
But victor thou shalt prove o'er all below,
Only seek strength above.

My Father, it is dark! Child, take my hand,
Cling close to me; I'll lead thee through the land;
Trust my all-seeing care; so shalt thou stand
'Midst glory bright above.

My footsteps seem to slide! Child, only raise
Thine eye to me; then in these slippery ways
I will hold up thy goings; thou shalt praise
Me for each step above.

O Father, I am weary! Child, lean thy head
Upon my breast. It was my love that spread
Thy rugged path. Hope on, till I have said,
"Rest, rest for aye, above."

A Joyous Way.

PHILIP DODDRIDGE.

Now let our voices join
  To form one pleasant song;
Ye pilgrims in Jehovah's ways,
  With music pass along.

How straight the path appears;
  How open and how fair!
No lurking gins to entrap our feet,
  No fierce destroyer there.

But flowers of Paradise
  In rich profusion spring;
The sun of glory gilds the path,
  And dear companions sing.

See Salem's golden spires
  In beauteous prospect rise,
And brighter crowns than mortals wear,
  Which sparkle through the skies.

All honor to his name
  Who drew the shining trace,
To Him who leads the wanderers on,
  And cheers them with his grace.

Reduce the nations, Lord;
  Teach all their kings thy ways,
That earth's full choir the notes may swell,
  And heaven resound the praise.

Dropping Down the River.

H. BONAR.

DROPPING down the troubled river,
  To the tranquil, tranquil shore,
Dropping down the misty river,
Time's willow-shaded river,
  To the spring-embosomed shore,
Where the sweet light shineth ever,
  And the sun goes down no more;
  O wondrous, wondrous shore!

Dropping down the winding river,
  To the wide and welcome sea;
Dropping down the narrow river,
Man's weary, wayward river,
  To the blue and ample sea,
Where no tempest wrecketh ever,
  Where the sky is fair and free;
  O joyous, joyous sea!

Dropping down the noisy river,
  To our peaceful, peaceful home;
Dropping down the turbid river,
Earth's bustling, crowded river,
  To our gentle, gentle home,
Where the rough roar riseth never,
  And the vexings cannot come;
  O loved and longed-for home!

Dropping down the eddying river,
  With a Helmsman true and tried;
Dropping down the perilous river,
Mortality's dark river,
  With a sure and heavenly Guide,
Even Him who, to deliver
  My soul from death, hath died;
  O Helmsman true and tried!

Dropping down the rapid river,
  To the dear and deathless land;
Dropping down the well-known river,
Life's swollen and rushing river,
  To the resurrection-land,
Where the living live forever,
  And the dead have joined the band;
  O fair and blessed land!

Through the Border Lands.

FATHER, into thy loving hands
My feeble spirit I commit,
While wandering in these border lands,
Until thy voice shall summon it.

Father, I would not dare to choose
A longer life, an earlier death;
I know not what my soul might lose
By shortened or protracted breath.

These border lands are calm and still,
And solemn are their silent shades;
And my heart welcomes them, until
The light of life's long evening fades.

I heard them spoken of with dread,
As fearful and unquiet places,
Shades where the living and the dead
Look sadly in each other's faces.

But since thy hand hath led me here,
And I have seen the border land,
Seen the dark river flowing near,
Stood on its brink, as now I stand,

There has been nothing to alarm
  My trembling soul; how could I fear
While thus encircled with thine arm?
  I never felt thee half so near.

What should appall me in a place
  That brings me hourly nearer thee?
When I may almost see thy face,
  Surely, 'tis here my soul would be.

They say the waves are dark and deep,
  That faith has perished in the river;
They speak of death with fear, and weep;
  Shall my soul perish? never, never!

I know that thou wilt never leave
  The soul that trembles while it clings
To thee; I know thou wilt achieve
  Its passage on thine outspread wings.

And since I first was brought so near
  The stream that flows to the Dead Sea,
I think that it has grown more clear
  And shallow than it used to be.

I cannot see the golden gate
  Unfolding yet to welcome me;
I cannot yet anticipate
  The joy of heaven's jubilee;

But I will calmly watch and pray,
  Until I hear my Saviour's voice,
Calling my happy soul away
  To see his glory and rejoice.

The Pilgrim's Prayer.

J. MONTGOMERY.

LORD, thy word is light;
Led by it aright,
When a pilgrim, like my fathers,
Life's last shadow round me gathers,
May its brightening ray
Shine to perfect day.

With my latest breath,
Overcoming death,
From the body disencumbered,
With thy saints in glory numbered,
Jesus, may I be
Found in peace with thee.

VI.

What is it to go to Heaven?

WHAT IS IT TO GO TO HEAVEN?

It is not Dying.

FROM THE FRENCH OF C. MALAN.

NO, no, it is not dying
To go unto our God,
The glowing earth forsaking,
Our journey homeward taking
Along the starry road.

No, no, it is not dying
Heaven's citizen to be,
The crown eternal wearing,
And rest unbroken sharing,
From care and conflict free.

No, no, it is not dying
To hear the precious word,
Receive a Father's blessing,
For evermore possessing
The favor of the Lord.

No, no, it is not dying
To wear a lordly crown,
Among God's people dwelling,
The glorious anthem swelling
Of Him whose love we own.

Oh, no, this is not dying,
Thou Saviour of mankind!
Streams there are overflowing
Of love, no hindrance knowing;
Dross only here we find.

Letting go Earth.

JOSIAH CONDER.

Oh, cling not, trembler, to life's fragile bark;
It fills — it soon must sink;
Look not below, where all is chill and dark;
'Tis agony to think
Of that wild waste; but look, oh, look above,
And see the outstretched arm of Love!

Cling not to this poor life; unlock thy clasp
Of fleeting, vapory air;
The world receding soon will mock thy grasp;
But let the wings of prayer
Take the blest breeze of heaven, and upward flee,
And life from God shall enter thee.

Oh fear not Him who walks the stormy wave;
'Tis not a spectre, but the Lord;
Trust thou in Him who overcame the grave,
Who holds in captive ward
The powers of hell. Heed not the monster grim,
Nor fear to go through death to Him.

Look not so fondly back on this false earth;
Let not hope linger here;
Say, would the worm forego its second birth,
Or the transition fear
That gives it wings to try a world unknown,
Although it wakes and mounts alone?

But thou art not alone; on either side
The portal friends stand guard,
And the kind spirits wait thy course to guide;
Why, why should it be hard
To trust our Maker with the soul he gave,
Or Him who died that soul to save?

Into his hands commit thy trembling spirit
Who gave his life for thine;
Guilty, fix all thy trust upon his merit;
To him thy heart resign;
Oh, give him love for love, and sweetly fall
Into his hands who is thy All!

Returning, not Departing.

H. BONAR.

I'M returning, not departing;
  My steps are homeward bound;
I quit the land of strangers
  For a home on native ground.

I am rising, and not setting;
  This is not night, but day;
Not in darkness, but in sunshine,
  Like a star, I fade away.

All is well with me forever;
  I do not fear to go;
My tide is but beginning
  Its bright, eternal flow.

I am leaving only shadows,
  For the true, and fair, and good;
I must not, cannot linger;
  I would not, though I could.

This is not death's dark portal;
  'Tis life's golden gate to me;
Link after link is broken,
  And I at last am free.

I am going to the angels,
  I am going to my God;
I know the hand that beckons;
  I see the holy road.

Why grieve me with your weeping?
  Your tears are all in vain;
An hour's farewell, beloved,
  And we shall meet again.

Jesus, thou wilt receive me,
  And welcome me above;
This sunshine which now fills me
  Is thine own smile of love.

Release from Prison.

THOMAS PARNELL.

DEATH's but a path that must be trod,
If man would ever pass to God;
A port of calms, a state of ease
From the rough rage of swelling seas.

As men who long in prison dwell,
With lamps that glimmer round the cell,
Whene'er their suffering years are run,
Spring forth to meet the glittering sun,

Such joy, though far transcending sense,
Have pious souls at parting hence;
On earth, and in the body placed,
A few and evil years they waste;

But, when their chains are cast aside,
See the bright scene unfolding wide,
Clap the glad wing, and tower away,
And mingle with the blaze of day.

Taking Wing.

B. B. THATCHER.

Earth is the spirit's rayless cell;
But then, as a bird soars home to the shade
Of the beautiful wood where its nest was made,
In bonds no more to dwell, —

So will its weary wing
Be spread for the skies when its toil is done,
And its breath flow free, as a bird's in the sun,
And the soft, fresh gales of spring.

Oh, not more sweet the tears
Of the dewy eve on the violet shed,
Than the dews of age on the hoary head
When it enters the eve of years.

Nor dearer, 'mid the foam
Of the far-off sea, and its stormy roar,
Is a breath of balm from the unseen shore
To him that weeps for home.

Wings, like a dove, to fly!
The spirit is faint with its feverish strife;
Oh for its home in the upper life!
When, when will death draw nigh?

Onward into Light.

RICHARD C. TRENCH.

OUR course is onward, onward into light;
What though the darkness gathereth amain?
Yet to return, or tarry, both are vain.
How tarry, when around us thick is night?
Whither return? What flower yet ever might,
In days of gloom, and cold, and stormy rain,
Enclose itself in its green bud again,
Hiding from wrath of tempest out of sight?
Courage! we travel through a darksome cave;
But still, as nearer to the light we draw,
Fresh gales will meet us from the upper air,
And wholesome dews of heaven our foreheads lave,
The darkness lighten more, till full of awe
We stand in the open sunshine, unaware.

Climbing the Stair.

ADELAIDE A. PROCTOR.

Dim shadows gather thickly round, and up the misty stair
they climb,
The cloudy stair that upward leads to where the closed
portals shine,
Round which the kneeling spirits wait the opening of the
golden gate.

And some with eager longing go, still pressing forward,
hand in hand,
And some, with weary step and slow, look back where
their beloved stand;
Yet up the misty stair they climb, led onward by the
angel Time.

As unseen hands roll back the doors, the light that floods
the very air
Is the dim shadow from within of the great glory hidden
there;
And morn and eve, and soon and late, the shadows pass
within the gate.

As, one by one, they enter in, and the dim portals close
once more,
The halo seems to linger round those kneeling closest to
the door:
The joy that lightened from that place shines still upon
the watcher's face.

The faint, low echo that we hear of far-off music seems
to fill
The silent air with love and fear, and the world's clamors
all grow still,
Until the portals close again, and leave us toiling on in
pain.

Complain not that the way is long; — what road is weary
that leads there?
But let the angel take thy hand, and lead thee up the
misty stair,
And then with beating heart await the opening of the
golden gate.

Passing the Gate.

THOMAS M'KELLAR.

THERE is a land immortal,
The beautiful of lands;
Beside the ancient portal
A sentry grimly stands;
He only can undo it,
And open wide the door;
And mortals who pass through it
Are mortals never more.

That glorious land is heaven,
  And Death the sentry grim;
The Lord, therefore, has given
  The opening keys to him;
And ransomed sinners, sighing
  And sorrowful for sin,
Do pass the gate in dying,
  And freely enter in.

Though dark and drear the passage
  That leadeth to the gate,
Yet grace comes with the message
  To souls that watch and wait;
And, at the time appointed,
  A messenger comes down,
And leads the Lord's anointed
  From cross to glory's crown.

Their sighs are lost in singing,
  They're blessed in their tears;
Their journey homeward winging,
  They leave to earth their fears;
Death like an angel seemeth;
  "We welcome thee," they cry;
Their face with glory beameth;
  'Tis life for them to die.

Bidding Good-Night.

FROM THE GERMAN.

I JOURNEY forth rejoicing
  From this dark vale of tears,
To heavenly joy and freedom,
  From earthly bonds and fears,
Where Christ our Lord shall gather
  All his redeemed again,
His kingdom to inherit;
                    Good-night till then.

Go to thy quiet resting,
  Poor tenement of clay;
From all thy pain and weakness
  I gladly haste away;
But still in faith confiding
  To find thee yet again,
All glorious and immortal;
                    Good-night till then.

Why thus so sadly weeping,
  Beloved ones of my heart?
The Lord is good and gracious,
  Though now he bids us part.
Oft have we met in gladness,
  And we shall meet again,
All sorrow left behind us;
                    Good-night till then.

I go to see his glory
  Whom we have loved below;
I go the blessed angels,
  The holy saints, to know;
Our lovely ones departed
  I go to find again,
And wait for you to join us;
  Good-night till then.

I hear the Saviour calling;
  The joyful hour has come;
The angel guards are ready
  To guide me to our home,
Where Christ our Lord shall gather
  All his redeemed again,
His kingdom to inherit;
  Good-night till then.

Bidding Farewell.

J. MONTGOMERY.

Let me go, the day is breaking;
  Dear companions, let me go;
We have spent a night of waking
  In the wilderness below;
Upward now I bend my way;
Part we here at break of day.

Let me go; I may not tarry,
  Wrestling thus with doubts and fears;
Angels wait my soul to carry
  Where my risen Lord appears;
Friends and kindred, weep not so;
If you love me, let me go.

We have travelled long together,
  Hand in hand and heart in heart,
Both through calm and stormy weather,
  And 'tis hard, 'tis hard to part;
Yet we must; farewell to you;
Answer, one and all, Adieu.

'Tis not darkness gathering round me
  Which withdraws me from your sight;
Walls of flesh no more can bound me;
  But, translated into light,
Like the lark on mounting wing,
Though unseen, you hear me sing.

Heaven's broad day hath o'er me broken,
  Far beyond earth's span of sky;
I am dead; nay, by this token
  Know that I have ceased to die.
Would you solve the mystery?
Come up hither, — come and see!

Floating to Glory.

JOHN WILSON.

A CLOUD lay cradled near the setting sun;
  A gleam of crimson tinged its braided snow;
Long had I watched the glory moving on,
  O'er the still radiance of the lake below;
Tranquil its spirit seemed, and floated slow;
  Even in its very motion there was rest;
While every breath of eve that chanced to blow
  Wafted the traveller to the beauteous west.
Emblem, methought, of the departed soul,
  To whose white robe the gleam of bliss is given,
And by the breath of mercy made to roll
  Right onward to the golden gates of heaven,
Where to the eye of faith it peaceful lies,
  And tells to man his glorious destinies.

Soaring to God.

AUGUSTUS M. TOPLADY.

DEATHLESS principle, arise!
Soar, thou native of the skies!
Pearl of price, by Jesus bought,
To his glorious likeness wrought,

Go to shine before his throne,
Deck his mediatorial crown;
Go, his triumphs to adorn;
Born for God, to God return.

Lo, he beckons from on high!
Fearless to his presence fly;
Thine the merit of his blood,
Thine the righteousness of God!
Angels, joyful to attend,
Hovering round thy pillow bend,
Wait to catch the signal given,
And escort thee quick to heaven.

Is thy earthly house distressed,
Willing to retain its guest?
'Tis not thou, but it, must die —
Fly, celestial tenant, fly!
Burst thy shackles! drop thy clay!
Sweetly breathe thyself away!
Singing, to thy crown remove,
Swift of wing, and fired with love!

Shudder not to pass the stream;
Venture all thy care on Him, —
Him, whose dying love and power
Stilled its tossing, hushed its roar;
Safe in the expanded wave,
Gentle as a summer's eve,

Not one object of his care
Ever suffered shipwreck there.

See the haven full in view;
Love divine shall bear thee through;
Trust to that propitious gale,
Weigh thine anchor, spread thy sail;
Saints in glory, perfect made,
Wait thy passage through the shade,
Ardent for thy coming o'er;
See, they throng the blissful shore!

Mount, their transports to improve:
Join the longing choir above;
Swiftly to their wish be given;
Kindle higher joy in heaven;—
Such the prospects that arise
To the dying Christian's eyes;
Such the glorious vista faith
Opens through the shades of death.

The Martyr's Triumph.

JOANNA BAILLIE.

A LONG farewell to sin and sorrow,
To beam of day and evening shade;
High in glory breaks our morrow,
With light that cannot fade.

While mortal flesh in flame is bleeding,
  For humble penitence and love,
Our Brother and our Lord is pleading
  At mercy's throne above.

We leave the hated and the hating,
  Existence sad in toil and strife;
The great, the good, the brave are waiting
  To hail our opening life.

Earth's faded sounds our ears forsaking,
  A moment's silence death shall be;
Then, to heaven's jubilee awaking,
  Faith ends in victory.

Sing with Me.

JAMES HOGG.

SING with me, sing with me,
Weeping brethren, sing with me!
For now an open heaven I see,
And a crown of glory laid for me.
How my soul this earth despises!
How my heart and spirit rises!
Bounding from the flesh I sever;
World of sin, adieu forever!

Sing with me, sing with me,
Friends in Jesus, sing with me!
All my sufferings, all my woe,
All my griefs, I here forego.
Farewell, terrors, sighing, grieving,
Praying, hearing, and believing,
Earthly trust and all its wrongings,
Earthly love and all its longings.

Sing with me, sing with me,
Blessed spirits, sing with me!
To the Lamb our songs shall be,
Through a glad eternity.
Farewell, earthly morn and even,
Sun, and moon, and stars of heaven;
Heavenly portals ope before me,
Welcome Christ in all his glory!

Singing Hallelujah.

H. H. MILMAN.

HALLELUJAH! Lord our God!
Now our earthly path is trod;
Passed are now our cares and fears,
And we quit this vale of tears.

Hallelujah! King of kings!
Now our spirits spread their wings
To the mansions of the blest,
To thy everlasting rest.

Hallelujah! Lord of lords!
Be our last and dying words,
Glory to our God above,
To our slaughterers peace and love.

A Smiling Infant.

CHRISTIAN EXAMINER.

'Tis dying; life is yielding place
  To that mysterious charm
Which spreads upon the troubled face
  A fixed, unchanging calm,
That deepens as the parting breath
Is gently sinking into death.

A thoughtful beauty rests the while
  Upon its snowy brow;
But those pale lips could never smile
  More radiantly than now;
And sure some heavenly dreams begin
To dawn upon the soul within.

Oh that those mildly conscious lips
  Were parted to reply,
To tell how death's severe eclipse
  Is passing from thine eye;
For living eye can never see
The change that death hath wrought in thee.

Perhaps thy sight is wandering far
  Throughout the kindled sky,
In tracing every infant star
  Amid the flames on high, —
Souls of the just, whose path is bent
Around the glorious firmament.

Perhaps thine eye is gazing down
  Upon the earth below,
Rejoicing to have gained thy crown,
  And hurried from its woe
To dwell beneath the throne of Him
Before whose glory heaven is dim.

Thy life, how cold it might have been,
  If days had grown to years!
How dark, how deeply stained with sin,
  With weariness and tears!
How happy thus to sink to rest,
So early numbered with the blest!

'Tis well, then, that the smile should lie
  Upon thy marble cheek;
It tells to our inquiring eye
  What words could never speak—
A revelation sweetly given
Of all that man can learn of heaven.

From Hovel to Heaven.

MRS. C. A. SOUTHEY.

TREAD softly; bow the head,
  In reverent silence bow;
No passing bell doth toll,
Yet an immortal soul
    Is passing now.

Stranger, how great soe'er,
  With lowly reverence bow;
There's one in that poor shed,
One by that wretched bed,
    Greater than thou.

Beneath that pauper's roof,
  Lo! Death doth keep his state;
Enter — no crowds attend;
Enter — no guards defend
    This palace gate.

That pavement damp and cold
  No whispering courtiers tread
One silent woman stands
Chafing, with pale, thin hands,
      A dying head.

No busy murmurs sound;
  An infant wail alone;
A sob suppressed — again
That short, deep gasp, and then
      The parting groan.

Oh change! Oh wondrous change!
  Burst are the prison bars!
This moment there, so low
In mortal prayer, — and now
      Beyond the stars!

Oh change! stupendous change!
  Here lies the senseless clod;
The soul from bondage breaks,
The new immortal wakes,
      Wakes with his God!

Going into Light.

HENRY VAUGHAN.

THEY are all gone into a world of light,
And I alone sit lingering here;
Their very memory is fair and bright,
And my sad thoughts doth clear.

It glows and glitters in my cloudy breast,
Like stars upon some gloomy grove,
Or those faint beams in which this hill is dressed,
After the sun's remove.

I see them walking in an air of glory,
Whose light doth trample on my days, —
My days, which are at best but dull and hoary,
Mere glimmering and decays.

O holy hope and high humility,
High as the heavens above!
These are your walks, and you have showed them me
To kindle my cold love.

Dear, beauteous Death, the jewel of the just,
Shining nowhere but in the dark!
What mysteries do lie beyond thy dust,
Could man outlook that mark!

He that hath found some fledged bird's nest may
know
At first sight if the bird be flown;
But what fair dell or grove he sings in now,
That is to him unknown.

And yet, as angels in some brighter dreams
Call to the soul when man doth sleep,
So some strange thoughts transcend our wonted
themes,
And into glory peep.

If a star were confined into a tomb,
Her captive flames must needs burn there;
But when the hand that locked her up gives room,
She'll shine through all the sphere.

O Father of eternal life, and all
Created glories under thee,
Resume thy spirit from this world of thrall
Into true liberty!

Either disperse these mists, which blot and fill
My perspective still as they pass;
Or else remove me hence unto that hill
Where I shall need no glass.

VII.

Who would not go to Heaven?

WHO WOULD NOT GO TO HEAVEN?

I. ASPIRATIONS AFTER HEAVEN.

Longing for Immortality.

MRS. ANNE STEELE.

SAD prisoners in a house of clay,
With sins, and griefs, and pains oppressed,
We groan the lingering hours away,
And wish and long to be released.

Nor is it liberty alone
Which prompts our restless, ardent sighs;
For immortality we groan,
For robes and mansions in the skies.

Eternal mansions, bright array!
Oh blest exchange, transporting thought,
Free from th' approaches of decay,
Or the least shadow of a spot!

There shall mortality no more
Its wide-extended empire boast,
Forgotten all its dreadful power,
In life's unbounded ocean lost.

Bright world of bliss, Oh could I see
One shining glimpse, one cheerful ray!
Fair dawn of immortality,
Break through these tottering walls of clay!

Jesus, in thy dear name I trust,
My light, my life, my Saviour God!
When this frail house dissolves in dust,
Oh raise me to thy bright abode!

Ardent Aspirations.

FROM THE LATIN OF CASIMIRE, BY WATTS.

THE beauty of my native land
Immortal love inspires;
I burn, I burn with strong desires,
And sigh, and wait the high command;
There glides the moon her shining way,
And shoots my heart through with a silver ray;
Upward my heart aspires:
A thousand lamps of golden light,
Hung high in vaulted azure, charm my sight,
And wink and beckon with their amorous fires.
O ye fair glories of my heavenly home,
Bright sentinels who guard my Father's court,
Where all the happy minds resort,
When will my Father's chariot come?

Must ye forever walk the ethereal round,
Forever see the mourner lie
An exile of the sky,
A prisoner of the ground?
Descend, some shining servants from on high,
Build me a hasty tomb;
A grassy turf will raise my head,
The neighboring lilies dress my bed,
And shed a cheap perfume.
Here I put off the chains of death
My soul too long has worn;
Friends, I forbid one groaning breath,
Or tear to wet my urn;
Raphael, behold me all undressed;
Here gently lay this flesh to rest;
Then mount, and lead the path unknown,
Swift I pursue thee, flaming guide, on pinions of
my own.

Why Tarry Here?

FROM THE SPANISH OF PONCE DE LEON, BY J. BOWRING.

WHEN yonder glorious sky,
Lighted with million lamps, I contemplate,
And turn my dazzled eye
To this vain mortal state,
All dim and visionary, mean and desolate,—

A mingled joy and grief
Fills all my soul with dark solicitude;
I find a short relief
In tears, whose torrents rude
Roll down my cheeks, or thoughts which thus intrude:

Thou so sublime abode,
Temple of light, and beauty's fairest shrine!
My soul, a spark of God,
Aspiring to thy seats divine,
Why, why is it condemned in this dull cell to pine?

Why should I ask in vain
For truth's pure lamp, and wander here alone,
Seeking, through toil and pain,
Light from the Eternal One,
Following a shadow still that glimmers and is gone?

Dreams and delusions play
With man; he thinks not of his mortal fate;
Death treads his silent way;
The earth turns round; and then, too late,
Man finds no beam is left of all his fancied state.

Rise from your sleep, vain men!
Look round, and ask if spirits born of heaven,
And bound to heaven again,
Were only lent or given
To be in this mean round of shades and follies driven.

Turn your unclouded eye
Up to yon bright, to yon eternal spheres,
And spurn the vanity
Of time's delusive years,
And all its flattering hopes, and all its frowning fears.

What is the ground ye tread,
But a mere point, compared with that vast space
Around, above you spread,
Where, in the Almighty's face,
The present, future, past, hold an eternal place?

List to the concert pure
Of yon harmonious, countless worlds of light!
See, in his orbit sure
Each takes his journey bright,
Led by an unseen hand through the vast maze of night.

But who to these can turn,
And weigh them 'gainst a weeping world like this,
Nor feel his spirit burn
To grasp so sweet a bliss,
And mourn that exile hard which here his portion is?

For there, and there alone,
Are peace, and joy, and never-dying love,—
There, on a splendid throne,
'Midst all those fires above,
In glories and delights which never wane nor move.

Oh wondrous blessedness,
Whose shadowy effluence hope o'er time can fling!
Day that shall never cease,—
No night there threatening,
No winter there to chill joy's ever-during spring.

Ye fields of changeless green,
Covered with living streams and fadeless flowers,
Thou paradise serene!
Eternal, joyful hours
My disembodied soul shall welcome in thy bowers.

Come, Sacred Song.

Come, sacred song, thy heaven of joy spread o'er me;
Thy golden-pinioned choir bring in thy train;
The keen delights that throng thy path restore me;
I will not fright thee from my side again.

Come at the morning hour, when life is gushing
Afresh from the great Fount of life above;
Its anthem let me hear, earth's sorrows hushing,
Turning my fevered soul to heaven's pure love.

Oh come, and breathe but one sweet strain of gladness,
To cheer my wearied spirit on its way;
Some wandering air of seraph's lyre, where sadness
No undertone can mingle with its lay.

Or let me hear that flood of music, pouring,
  Like the deep voice of thousand oceans' flow,
From the great multitude of saints adoring
  In heaven's high court, and in the church below.

Or let me hear thee, at the altar kneeling,
  As when He sung of old that hymn divine,
To loving hearts eternal joys revealing,
  Where mortal forms in robes immortal shine.

My spirit lives upon thy heavenly numbers,
  And I companion of thy way would be,
Where thy pure beams illume the infant's slumbers,
  Or the high places of eternity.

Come, sacred song, at the cool hour of evening
  Thy strains of joy pour on its sacred rest;
Let my repose in life and death, like heaven,
  All blissful be with anthems of the blest.

Come at the silent hour of night, and bear me
  To your pure world, where discords never come;
Tune my dark soul; exalt, refine, prepare me
  To sing with thee in thy celestial home.

Enraptured Contemplation.

EDMUND SPENSER.

THEY see such admirable things,
As carries them into an exstasy,
And heare such heavenly notes and carolings
Of God's high praise, that filles the brasen sky,
And feele such joy and pleasure inwardly,
That maketh them all worldly cares forget,
And onely think on that before them set.

Ne from henceforth doth any fleshly sense,
Or idle thought of earthly things, remaine;
But all that earst seemd sweet seemes now offense,
And all that pleased earst now seemes to paine;
Their ioy, their comfort, their desire, their gaine,
Is fixed all on that which now they see;
All other sights but fayned shadows bee.

And that fair lampe which useth to enflame
The hearts of men with selfe-consuming fyre,
Thenceforth seemes fowle, and full of sinfull blame;
And all that pompe to which proud minds aspyre,
By name of honor, and so much desyre,
Seemes to them basenesse, and all riches drosse,
And all mirth sadnesse, and all lucre losse.

So full their eyes are of that glorious sight,
  And senses fraught with such satietie,
That in nought else on earth they can delight,
  But in the aspect of that felicitie
  Which they have written in theyr inward ey,
  On which they feed, and in theyr fastened mynd
  All happie ioy and full contentment fynd.

Ah, then, my hungry soule, which long hast fed
  On idle fancies of thy foolish thought,
And, with false beautie's flattering bait misled,
  Hast after vaine, deceitfull shadowes sought,
  Which all are fled, and now have left thee nought
  But late repentance through thy follies brief;
  Ah! cease to gaze on matter of thy grief,

And looke at last up to that soveraine Light
  From whose pure beams all perfect beauty springs,
That kindleth love in every godly spright,
  Even the love of God; which loathing brings
  Of this vile world and these gay-seeming things;
  With whose sweet pleasures being so possest,
  Thy straying thoughts henceforth forever rest.

Salem Espied.

FROM THE LATIN OF ZUINGER, BY MERRICK.

WHAT joy, while thus I view the day
That warns my thirsting soul away,
  What transports fill my breast!
For, lo! my great Redeemer's power
Unfolds the everlasting door,
  And leads me to his rest.

The festive morn, my God, is come
That calls me to the hallowed dome,
  Thy presence to adore;
My feet the summons shall attend,
With willing steps thy courts ascend,
  And tread th' ethereal floor.

E'en now to my expecting eyes
The heaven-built towers of Salem rise;
  E'en now, with glad survey,
I view her mansions, that contain
Th' angelic forms, an awful train,
  And shine with cloudless day.

Hither, from earth's remotest end,
Lo! the redeemed of God ascend,
  Their tribute hither bring;
Here, crowned with everlasting joy,
In hymns of praise their tongues employ,
  And hail the immortal King; —

Great Salem's King, who bids each state
On her decrees dependent wait;
  In her, ere time begun,
High on eternal base upreared,
His hands the regal seat prepared
  For Jesse's favored Son.

Mother of cities! o'er thy head
See Peace, with healing wings outspread,
  Delighted fix her stay;
How blest who calls himself thy friend;
Success his labors shall attend,
  And safety guard his way.

Thy walls, remote from hostile fear,
Nor the loud voice of tumult hear,
  Nor war's wild wastes deplore;
There smiling Plenty takes her stand,
And in thy courts with lavish hand
  Has poured forth all her store.

Let me, blest seat, my name behold
Among thy citizens enrolled,
  In thee forever dwell;
Let Charity my steps attend,
My sole companion and my friend,
  And Faith and Hope farewell.

Jerusalem, thou City Fair and High.

FROM THE GERMAN OF J. M. MEYFART, BY MISS C. WINKWORTH.

JERUSALEM, thou city fair and high,
Would God I were in thee!
My longing heart fain, fain to thee would fly, —
It will not stay with me;
Far over vale and mountain,
Far over field and plain,
It hastes to seek its Fountain,
And quit this world of pain.

Oh happy day, and yet far happier hour,
When wilt thou come at last,
When, fearless, to my Father's love and power,
Whose promise standeth fast,
My soul I gladly render?
For surely will his hand
Lead her, with guidance tender,
To heaven, her fatherland.

A moment's space, and gently, wondrously,
Released from earthly ties,
The fiery chariot bears her up to thee,
Through all these lower skies,
To yonder shining regions,
While down to meet her come
The blessed angel legions,
And bid her welcome home.

Oh hail, thou glorious city! now unfold
  The gates of grace to me!
How many a time I longed for thee of old,
  Ere yet I was set free
  From yon dark life of sadness,
    Yon world of shadowy nought,
  And God had given the gladness,
    The heritage I sought.

Oh what the nation, what the glorious host,
  Comes sweeping swiftly down?
The chosen ones on earth who wrought the most,
  The church's brightest crown,
  Our Lord hath sent to meet me,
    As in the far-off years
  Their words oft came to greet me
    In yonder land of tears.

The patriarchs' and prophets' noble train,
  With all Christ's followers true,
Who bore the cross, and could the worst disdain
  That tyrants dared to do,
  I see them shine forever,
    All-glorious as the sun,
  'Mid light that fadeth never,
    Their perfect freedom won.

And when within that lovely Paradise
At last I safely dwell,
From out my blissful soul what songs shall rise,
What joy my lips shall tell,
While holy saints are singing
Hosannas o'er and o'er,
Pure hallelujahs ringing
Around me evermore.

Innumerous choirs before the shining throne
Their joyful anthems raise,
Till heaven's glad halls are echoing with the tone
Of that great hymn of praise,
And all its host rejoices,
And all its blessed throng
Unite their myriad voices
In one eternal song.

I am Weary.

I AM weary of straying; oh, fain would I rest
In the far-distant land of the pure and the blest,
Where sin can no longer her blandishments spread,
And fears and temptations forever have fled.

I am weary of hoping, where hope is untrue,
As fair, but as fleeting, as morning's bright dew;
I long for that land whose blest promise alone
Is changeless and sure as eternity's throne.

I am weary of sighing o'er sorrows of earth,
O'er joy's glowing visions that fade at their birth,
O'er the pangs of the loved, that we cannot assuage,
O'er the blightings of youth, and the weakness of age.

I am weary of loving what passes away;
The sweetest, the dearest, alas! may not stay;
I long for that land where these partings are o'er,
And death and the tomb can divide hearts no more.

I am weary, my Saviour, of grieving thy love;
Oh, when shall I rest in thy presence above?
I am weary, but, oh! let me never repine,
While thy word, and thy love, and thy promise, are
mine.

I would not Live Alway.

W. A. MUHLENBERG.

I WOULD not live alway, live alway below;
Oh, no, I'll not linger when bidden to go;
The days of our pilgrimage granted us here
Are enough for life's woes, full enough for its cheer.

Would I shrink from the path which the prophets of
God,
Apostles and martyrs, so joyously trod?
While brethren and friends are all hastening home,
Like a spirit unblest o'er the earth would I roam?

I would not live alway; I ask not to stay
Where storm after storm rises o'er the dark way;
Where, seeking for peace, we but hover around,
Like the patriarch's bird, and no resting is found;
Where Hope, when she paints her gay bow in the air,
Leaves its brilliance to fade in the night of despair;
And joy's fleeting angel ne'er sheds a glad ray,
Save the gleam of the plumage that bears him away.

I would not live alway, thus fettered by sin,
Temptation without, and corruption within;
In a moment of strength if I sever the chain,
Scarce the victory's mine ere I'm captive again;
E'en the rapture of pardon is mingled with fears,
And the cup of thanksgiving with penitent tears;
The festival trump calls for jubilant songs,
And my spirit her own miserere prolongs.

I would not live alway; no, welcome the tomb!
Immortality's lamp burns there bright 'mid the gloom;
There, too, is the pillow where Christ bowed his head;
Oh, soft are the slumbers of that holy bed!

And then the glad dawn soon to follow that night,
When the sunrise of glory shall beam on my sight,
When the full matin song, as the sleepers arise
To shout in the morning, shall peal through the skies.

Who, who would live alway, away from his God,
Away from yon heaven, that blissful abode,
Where the rivers of pleasure flow o'er the bright
plains,
And the noontide of glory eternally reigns;
Where the saints of all ages in harmony meet,
Their Saviour and brethren transported to greet;
While the songs of salvation unceasingly roll,
And the smile of the Lord is the feast of the soul?

That heavenly music, what is it I hear?
The notes of the harp ring sweet on the ear;
And see, soft unfolding, those portals of gold;
The King, all arrayed in his beauty, behold.
Oh give me, Oh give me the wings of a dove;
Let me hasten my flight to those mansions above;
Ay, 'tis now that my soul on swift pinions would
soar,
And in ecstasy bid earth adieu evermore!

In Haste to be Gone.

H. BONAR.

BEYOND the hills where suns go down,
And brightly beckon as they go,
I see the land of fair renown,
The land which I so soon shall know.

Above the dissonance of time,
And discord of its angry words,
I hear the everlasting chime,
The music of unjarring chords.

I bid it welcome, and my haste
To join it cannot brook delay;
Oh song of morning, come at last,
And ye who sing it, come away!

Oh song of light, and dawn, and bliss,
Sound over earth, and fill these skies;
Nor ever, ever, ever cease
Thy soul-entrancing melodies;—

Glad song of this disburdened earth,
Which holy voices then shall sing,
Praise for creation's second birth,
And glory to creation's King.

My Soul, go boldly Forth.

BAXTER.

My soul, go boldly forth,
Forsake this sinful earth;
What hath it been to thee
        But pain and sorrow?
And think'st thou it will be
        Better to-morrow?

Why art thou for delay?
Thou cam'st not here to stay;
What tak'st thou for thy part
        But heavenly pleasure?
Where then should be thy heart
        But where's thy treasure?

Thy God, thy Head, 's above;
There is a world of love;
Mansions there purchased are
        By Christ's own merit;
For there he doth prepare
        Thee by his Spirit.

Lord Jesus, take my spirit;
I trust thy love and merit:
Take home thy wandering sheep,
        For thou has sought it;
My soul in safety keep,
        For thou hast bought it.

Death Welcomed.

FROM THE GERMAN OF J. G. ALBINUS, BY H. MILLS.

ALL must die! there's no redemption;
Flesh! 'tis all alike but grass!
None that live can plead exemption;
Saints through death to glory pass.
This vile body here must perish
Ere, immortal, it can cherish
Holy joys, the free reward
For the ransomed of the Lord.

Life on earth can I then covet
Longer than my God shall please?
When above he would remove it,
I will greet the soul's release.
For, through what my Saviour suffered,
Freedom from the curse is offered;
He has promised, and to faith
Gives the victory over death.

Death — for me the Saviour bore it;
Dying, won for me the prize:
Life — he will in bliss restore it;
Shall I not then joyful rise
From this world of sin and anguish
To that world for which I languish,
There the Three in One to praise,
With his saints, through endless days?

Happy spirits, ever living,
  Thousand thousands all as one,
Robed in light, their worship giving,
  There rejoice before the throne.
There the seraphim are shining,
Evermore in chorus joining—
  "Holy! holy! holy Lord!
  Be thy holy name adored!"

Worthies, there, of sacred story,
  Prophets, patriarchs, are met;
There, apostles, too, in glory
  Fill their thrones by Jesus set;
All the saints that have ascended,
Age on age through time extended,
  There in blissful concert sing
  Hallelujahs to their King.

O Jerusalem, thou fairest!
  In thy King how greatly blest!
Praising thou his splendor sharest
  Through thy streets of holy rest:
Joy and peace, in thee united,
By no fear of change are blighted,
  Balmy fragrance cheers the day,
  Which no night shall drive away.

Yes, methinks I now behold it,
That fair city of delight;
Now the robe — around me fold it,
Robe of dazzling, purest white;
There, a crown of victory wearing,
There, before the throne appearing,
Mingle with the heirs of bliss,
Where hosannas never cease.

World, Farewell.

FROM THE GERMAN OF J. G. ALBINUS, BY MISS C. WINKWORTH.

World, farewell! of thee I'm tired,
Now toward heaven my way I take;
There is peace the long-desired,
Lofty calm that nought can break.
World, with thee is war and strife,
Thou with cheating hopes art rife;
But in heaven is no alloy,
Only peace and love and joy.

When I reach that home of gladness,
I shall feel no more this load,
Feel no sickness, want, or sadness,
Resting in the arms of God.

In the world woes follow fast,
And a bitter death comes last,
But in heaven shall nought destroy
Endless peace and love and joy.

What are earthly joys? a weary
  Chase of mist, or wind-borne foam.
On this desert black and dreary
  Sins and vices have their home;
Thine, O world, are war and strife,
Mocking pleasures, dying life;
But in heaven is no annoy,
Only peace, and love, and joy.

Oh, the music and the singing
  Of the host redeemed by love!
Oh, the hallelujahs ringing
  Through the halls of light above!
Thine, O world, the scornful sneer,
Misery thy reward, and fear;
But in heaven is no annoy,
Only peace, and love, and joy.

Here is nought but care and mourning;
  Comes a joy, it will not stay;
Fairly shines the sun at dawning,
  Night will soon o'ercloud the day:

World, with thee we weep and pine;
Gnawing care and grief are thine;
But in heaven is no alloy,
Only peace, and love, and joy.

Onward, then; not long I wander,
  Ere my Saviour comes for me,
And with him abiding yonder,
  All his glory I shall see;
For there's nought but sorrow here,
Toil, and pain, and many a fear;
But in heaven is no annoy,
Only peace, and love, and joy.

Well for him whom death has landed
  Safely on yon blessed shore,
Where, in joyful worship banded,
  Sing the faithful evermore;
For the world hath strife and war;
All her works and hopes they mar;
But in heaven is no annoy,
Only peace, and love, and joy.

Time, thou speedest on but slowly;
  Hours, how tardy is your pace,
Ere with Him, the High and Holy,
  I hold converse, face to face;

World, with partings thou art rife,
Filled with tears, and storms, and strife;
But in heaven can nought destroy
Endless peace, and love, and joy.

Therefore will I now prepare me,
  That my work may stand his doom,
And, when all is sinking round me,
  I may hear, not Go, but Come!
World, the voice of grief is here,
Outward seeming, care, and fear;
But in heaven is no alloy,
Only peace, and love, and joy.

Let me Depart.

LADY FLORA HASTINGS.

GRIEVE not that I die young; is it not well
  To pass away ere life hath lost its brightness?
Bind me no longer, sisters, with the spell
Of love and your kind words. List ye to me:
Here I am blessed, but I would be more free;
  I would go forth in all my spirit's lightness:
                    Let me depart.

Ah! who would linger till bright eyes grow dim,
  Kind voices mute, and faithful bosoms cold?
Till carking care, and coil, and anguish grim,
Cast their dark shadows o'er this faëry world;
Till fancy's many-colored wings are furled,
  And all, save the proud spirit, waxeth old?
            I would depart.

Thus would I pass away, yielding my soul
  A joyous thank-offering to Him who gave
That soul to be, those starry orbs to roll;
Thus, thus exultingly would I depart,
Song on my lips, ecstasy in my heart;
  Sisters, sweet sisters, bear me to my grave:
            Let me depart.

II. LONGING TO BE WITH JESUS.

Or Take me Up to Thee.

GEORGE HERBERT.

COME, Lord, my head doth burn, my heart is sick,
Whilst thou dost ever, ever stay;
Thy long deferrings wound me to the quick;
My spirit gaspeth night and day:
Oh, show thyself to me,
Or take me up to thee!

Yet, if thou stayest still, why must I stay?
My God, what is this world to me,
This world of woe? Hence, all ye clouds, away,
Away; I must get up and see:
Oh, show thyself to me,
Or take me up to thee!

With one small sigh thou gav'st me th' other day
I blasted all the joys about me;
And, scowling on them, as they pined away,
"Now come again," said I, "and flout me:"
Oh, show thyself to me,
Or take me up to thee!

Nothing but drought and dearth, but bush and brake,
  Which way soe'er I look, I see;
Some may dream merrily; but, when they wake,
  They dress themselves, and come to thee:
    Oh, show thyself to me,
    Or take me up to thee!

We talk of harvests; there are no such things
  But when we leave our corn and hay;
There is no fruitful year but that which brings
  The last and loved, though dreadful day:
    Oh, show thyself to me,
    Or take me up to thee!

Oh, loose this frame, this knot of man untie,
  That my free soul may use her wing,
Which now is pinioned with mortality,
  As an entangled, hampered thing!
    Oh, show thyself to me,
    Or take me up to thee!

What have I left, that I should stay and groan?
  The most of me to heaven is fled;
My thoughts and joys are all packed up and gone,
  And for their old acquaintance plead:
    Oh, show thyself to me,
    Or take me up to thee!

"Come, dearest Lord, pass not this holy season,"
My flesh, and bones, and joints do pray;
And e'en my verse, when, by the rhyme and reason,
The word is Stay, says ever, Come:
Oh, show thyself to me,
Or take me up to thee!

My Redeemer Lives.

FROM THE GERMAN OF LOUISA HENRIETTA, WIFE OF FREDERICK WILLIAM, ELECTOR OF BRANDENBURG, BY J. S. LOPES.

JESUS, who is all my trust,
Jesus, my Redeemer, lives;
Though my body sink in dust,
This assurance comfort gives:
Death's long night I need not fear,
When I know that He is near.

Jesus, my Redeemer, lives;
I with him shall live on high;
Life to me his promise gives;
Why, then, should I fear to die?
Can my glorious risen Head
Leave his members with the dead?

No; too strong the sacred band
  That unites my soul to him;
While I clasp his gracious hand,
  Faith and hope can ne'er grow dim;
Death itself shall never part
My Redeemer from my heart.

Born of flesh, my mortal frame
  Must, I know, in dust decay;
But my Lord that dust shall claim,
  And his voice shall wake the clay;
Then shall I in glory rise
To a mansion in the skies.

Then, as faith assurance gives,
  Him, my God, shall I behold,
Know that my Redeemer lives,
  And the grave shall lose its hold;
Then my flesh revived shall stand
Evermore at Christ's right hand.

There these eyes with raptured gaze
  My Redeemer's form shall know;
'Mid the bright, unclouded rays
  Of his love my soul shall glow;
Nought of weakness shall remain,
Purged away each earthly stain.

Here I suffer, weep, and groan;
  There I shall in glory shine;
Here an earthly body sown,
  There a heavenly form is mine;
Mortal, in the dust I lie,
Spirit, I ascend on high.

Let the thought our spirits cheer,
  Jesus bears us on our way;
Give no place to grief or fear;
  Calm in death, expect the day
When the last loud trumpet's sound
Calls you from beneath the ground.

Smiling greet the darksome tomb;
  Look not on the grave with fear;
Christ shall dissipate its gloom;
  You shall meet him in the air;
Every foe that once could try
Vanquished at your feet shall lie.

Seek then now your soul to raise
  From the earth and things below;
Consecrated to his praise
  To whose courts you long to go,
Thither now your heart impel
Where you would forever dwell.

Christ my All.

FROM THE GERMAN OF PAUL GERHARD.

O Christ, how good and fair
Will be my portion where
Thine eyes on me shall rest,
And make me fully blest,
When from this narrow earth
To thee I shall spring forth!

What joy, unmixed and full,
Thou Treasure of the soul,
When, in that home above,
Thy heart speaks out its love
To all made one with thee,
My brothers, Lord, and me!

What glorious light will shine
Forth from thy face divine,
Which in that life untold
Then first I shall behold!
How will thy goodness free
Fill me with ecstasy!

Lips, whence such words have streamed,
Eyes, whence such pity beamed,
Side, wounded once for me,
All, all I then shall see,
With reverent rapture greet
Thy pierced hands and feet!

Ah, Jesus, my "good part,"
How will my mind and heart
Vibrate with rapture through,
And all my soul grow new,
When thou, with smiles of love,
Openest those gates above!

"Come," thou wilt say, "blest child,
Taste pleasures undefiled,
And see the gifts, how fair,
My Father's hands prepare;
Pasture thine heart forever
In joy that fadeth never."

O thou poor, passing earth!
What are thy treasures worth
Beside those heavenly crowns,
And more than golden thrones,
Which Christ hath treasured there
For those who please him here?

This is the angels' land,
Where all the blessed stand;
Here I hear nought but singing,
See all with gladness springing;
Here is no cross, no sorrow,
No parting on the morrow.

When shall that joy begin?
When wilt thou call me in?
Thou knowest; but my feet
Press onward thee to meet,
And my heart, day by day,
Bears me to thee away.

Longing for His Voice.

CHARLOTTE ELLIOTT.

THERE are refreshments sweeter far than sleep,
Though its soft power
Might gladly close the vigils I now keep
From hour to hour,
And hush these vain imaginings to rest,
Which silence in my heart its dearest guest.

Oh, I have heard his voice, his voice of love,
In the still night,
Sweet as the songs from seraph hearts above,
Tranced in delight!
It haunts my memory, lives within my heart,
And makes me long, yea, languish to depart.

Those who have heard it once can ne'er forget
That voice divine;
With it compared, earth's accents are not sweet.
My God, I pine
A dweller in those palaces to be,
Where I shall hear it through eternity.

Then I shall ne'er be harassed by the din
Of earthly thought;
All will be holy and serene within;
My spirit, fraught
With deepest reverence, with intense desire,
Will listen to that voice, and never tire.

Oh that I had Wings like a Dove!

My soul, amid this stormy world,
Is like some fluttered dove,
And fain would be as swift of wing,
To flee to Him I love.

The cords that bound my heart to earth
Are broken by his hand;
Before his cross I found myself,
A stranger in the land.

That visage marred, those sorrows deep,
The vinegar and gall,
Were Jesus' golden chains of love,
His captive to enthrall.

My heart is with him on his throne
And ill can brook delay,
Each moment listening for the voice,
"Rise up, and come away."

With hope deferred, oft sick and faint,
"Why tarries he?" I cry;
And should my Saviour chide my haste,
Sure I could make reply, —

May not an exile, Lord, desire
His own sweet land to see?
May not a captive seek release,
A prisoner to be free?

A child, when far away, may long
For home and kindred dear,
And she that waits her absent Lord
May sigh till he appear.

I would, my Lord and Saviour, know
That which no measure knows;
Would search the mystery of thy love,
The depth of all thy woes.

I want to be There.

DE FLEURY.

Ye angels who stand round the throne,
  And view my Immanuel's face,
In rapturous songs make him known;
  Tune, tune your soft harps to his praise;
He formed you the spirits you are,
  So happy, so noble, so good;
When others sunk down in despair,
  Confirmed by his power ye stood.

Ye saints, who stand nearer than they,
  And cast your bright crowns at his feet,
His grace and his glory display,
  And all his rich mercy repeat;
He snatched you from hell and the grave;
  He ransomed from death and despair;
For you he was mighty to save,
  Almighty to bring you safe there.

Oh, when will the moment appear
  When I shall unite in your song?
I'm weary of lingering here,
  And I to your Saviour belong;
I'm fettered and chained up in clay;
  I struggle and pant to be free;
I long to be soaring away,
  My God and my Saviour to see.

I want to put on my attire,
  Washed white in the blood of the Lamb;
I want to be one of your choir,
  And tune my sweet harp to his name;
I want, oh, I want to be there,
  Where sorrow and sin bid adieu,
Your joy and your friendship to share,
  To wonder and worship with you!

To be with Christ far Better.

Away with our sorrow and fear;
  We soon shall have entered our home;
The city of saints shall appear,
  The day of eternity come;
From earth we shall quickly remove,
  To dwell in a native abode,
In mansions of glory above,
  Prepared of our Father and God.

Ah! who upon earth can conceive
  The bliss that in heaven they'll share?
And who this dark world would not leave,
  And cheerfully seek to be there,

Where Christ is the Light and the Sun,
  And we by reflection shall shine,
With him everlastingly one,
  And bright in effulgence divine?

'Tis good at thy word to be here;
  'Tis better in thee to be gone,
And see thee in glory appear,
  And rise to a share in thy throne;
All tears will be wiped from our eyes,
  When thee we behold in the cloud,
And echo the joys of the skies,
  And shout to the trumpet of God.

While on the Verge of Life I Stand.

PHILIP DODDRIDGE.

While on the verge of life I stand,
And view the scenes on either hand,
My spirit struggles with its clay,
And longs to wing its flight away.

Where Jesus dwells my soul would be;
It faints my much-loved Lord to see;
Earth, twine no more about my heart,
For 'tis far better to depart.

Come, ye angelic envoys, come,
And lead the willing pilgrim home;
Ye know the way to Jesus' throne,
Source of my joys and of your own.

That blessed interview how sweet,
To fall transported at his feet;
Raised in his arms, to view his face,
Through the full beamings of his grace;

To see heaven's shining courtiers round,
Each with immortal glories crowned,
And, while his form in each I trace,
Beloved and loving all to embrace;

As with a seraph's voice to sing;
To fly as on a cherub's wing;
Performing, with unwearied hands,
A present Saviour's high commands!

Yet, with these prospects full in sight,
I'll wait thy signal for my flight;
For, while thy service I pursue,
I find my heaven begun below.

I Long to Behold Him Arrayed.

CHARLES WESLEY.

I LONG to behold him arrayed
  With glory and light from above,
The King in his beauty displayed,
  His beauty of holiest love;
I languish and sigh to be there,
  Where Jesus has fixed his abode;
Oh, when shall we meet in the air,
  And fly to the mountain of God?

With him I on Zion shall stand,
  For Jesus hath spoken the word,
The breadth of Immanuel's land
  Survey by the light of my Lord;
But when, on thy bosom reclined,
  Thy face I am strengthened to see,
My fulness of rapture I find,
  My heaven of heavens, in thee.

How happy the people that dwell
  Secure in the city above!
No pain the inhabitants feel,
  No sickness or sorrow shall prove.
Physician of souls, unto me
  Forgiveness and holiness give;
And then from the body set free,
  And then to the city receive!

Christ the Glory of Heaven.

MRS. ANNE STEELE.

OH for the wings of faith and love,
To bear my thoughts and hopes above
These little scenes of care!
Above these gloomy mists which rise,
And pain my heart, and cloud my eyes,
To see the dawn of heavenly day, and breathe celestial air.

Yet higher would I stretch my flight,
And reach the sacred courts of light,
Where my Redeemer reigns;
Far-beaming from his radiant throne,
Immortal splendors, joys unknown,
With never-fading lustre, shine o'er all the blissful plains.

Ten thousand times ten thousand tongues
There join in rapture-breathing songs,
And tune the golden lyre
To Jesus, their exalted Lord;
Dear name, how loved, and how adored!
His charms awake the heavenly strain, and every note inspire.

No short-lived pleasure there beguiles,
But perfect bliss forever smiles,
With undeclining ray;
Thither my thoughts would fain ascend,
But, ah! to dust and earth they bend,
Fettered with empty vanities, and chained to lifeless clay.

Dear Lord, and shall I ever be
So far from bliss, so far from thee,
An exile from the sky?
Oh break these chains, my wishes fire,
And upward bid my heart aspire;
Without thy aid I cannot rise; oh give me wings to fly!

Christ altogether Lovely.

MRS. ANNE STEELE.

Should nature's charms, to please the eye,
In sweet assemblage join,
All nature's charms would droop and die,
Jesus, compared with thine.

Vain were her fairest beams displayed,
And vain her blooming store;
Even brightness languishes to shade,
And beauty is no more.

But ah, how far from mortal sight
  The Lord of glory dwells!
A veil of interposing night
  His radiant face conceals.

Oh could my longing spirit rise
  On strong, immortal wing,
And reach thy palace in the skies,
  My Saviour and my King!

There myriads worship at thy feet,
  And there — divine employ —
The triumphs of thy love repeat,
  In songs of endless joy.

Thy presence beams eternal day
  O'er all the blissful place;
Who would not drop this load of clay
  And die to see thy face?

To Jesus the Crown of my Hope.

WM. COWPER.

To Jesus, the crown of my hope,
  My soul is in haste to be gone;
Oh bear me, ye cherubim, up,
  And waft me away to his throne!

My Saviour, whom absent I love,
  Whom, not having seen, I adore,
Whose name is exalted above
  All glory, dominion, and power;

Dissolve thou these bonds, that detain
  My soul from her portion in thee;
Ah, strike off this adamant chain,
  And make me eternally free!

When that happy era begins,
  When arrayed in thy glories I shine,
Nor grieve any more by my sins
  The bosom on which I recline,—

Oh then shall the veil be removed,
  And round me thy brightness be poured;
I shall meet him whom absent I loved,
  I shall see whom unseen I adored.

And then never more shall the fears,
  The trials, temptations, and woes,
Which darken this valley of tears,
  Intrude on my blissful repose.

Or, if yet remembered above,
  Remembrance no sadness shall raise;
They will be but new signs of thy love,
  New themes for my wonder and praise.

Thus the strokes which from sin and from pain
Shall set me eternally free,
Will but strengthen and rivet the chain
Which binds me, my Saviour, to thee.

When will He Come?

HENRY VAUGHAN.

Ah! what time wilt thou come? when shall that crie,
"The Bridegroom's coming!" fill the sky?

Shall it in the evening run,
When our words and works are done?
Or will thy all-surprising light
Break at midnight,
When either sleep, or some dark pleasure,
Possesseth mad man without measure?
Or shall these early fragrant hours
Unlock thy bowers,
And, with their blush of light, descry
Thy locks crowned with eternitie?
Indeed, it is the only time
That with thy glory doth best chime:
All now are stirring; every field
Full hymns doth yield;
The whole creation shakes off night,
And for thy shadow looks the light;

Stars now vanish without number;
Sleepie planets set and slumber;
The pursie clouds disband and scatter;
All expect some sudden matter;
Not one beam triumphs, but from far
That Morning Star.
Oh, at what time soever Thou,
Unknown to us, the heavens wilt bow,
And, with thy angels in the van,
Descend to judge poor careless man,
Grant, ...
As this restless, vocal spring
All day and night doth run and sing,
And though here born, yet is acquainted
Elsewhere, and flowing keeps untainted;
So let me, all my busie age,
In thy free services engage;
And though, while here, of force I must
Have commerce sometimes with poor dust,
And in my flesh, though vile and low,
As this doth in her channel flow,
Yet let my course, my aim, my love,
And chief acquaintance, be above;
So, when that day and hour shall come
In which thyself wilt be the sun,
Thou'lt find me dressed and on my way,
Watching the break of thy great day.

When, Lord, oh when shall We?

JEREMY TAYLOR.

When, Lord, oh when shall we
Our dear Salvation see?
  Arise, arise;
  Our fainting eyes
Have longed all night, and 'twas a long one, too.
Man never yet could say
He saw more than one day,
  One day of Eden's seven;
The guilty hours, there blasted with the breath
Of sin and death,
Have ever since worn a nocturnal hue;
But thou hast given us hopes that we,
At length, another day shall see,
  Wherein each vile, neglected place,
  Gilt with the aspect of thy face,
Shall be, like that, the porch and gate of heaven.
  How long, dear God, how long?
  See how the nations throng;
  All human kind,
  Knit and combined
Into one body, look for thee their head.
  Pity our multitude;
  Lord, we are vile and rude,
  Headless and senseless, without thee,

Of all things but the want of thy blest face;
Oh haste apace,
  And thy bright self to this our body wed,
  That, through the influx of thy power,
  Each part, that erst confusion wore,
  May put on order, and appear
  Spruce, as the childhood of the year,
When thou to it shalt so united be. Amen.

When shall thy Lovely Face be Seen?

ISAAC WATTS.

WHEN shall thy lovely face be seen?
  When shall our eyes behold our God?
What lengths of distance lie between,
  And hills of guilt, a heavy load!

Our months are ages of delay,
  And slowly every minute wears;
Fly, winged time, and roll away
  These tedious rounds of sluggish years.

Ye heavenly gates, loose all your chains;
  Let the eternal pillars bow;
Blest Saviour, cleave the starry plains,
  And make the crystal mountains flow.

Hark, how thy saints unite their cries,
And pray, and wait the general doom;
Come thou, the Soul of all our joys,
Thou, the Desire of nations, come.

Our spirits shake their eager wings,
And burn to meet thy flying throne;
We rise away from mortal things
T' attend thy shining chariot down.

Now let our cheerful eyes survey
The blazing earth and melting hills,
And smile to see the lightnings play,
And flash along before thy wheels.

Oh for a shout of violent joys
To join the trumpet's thundering sound!
The angel herald shakes the skies,
Awakes the graves, and tears the ground.

Ye slumbering saints, a heavenly host
Stands waiting at your gaping tombs;
Let every sacred sleeping dust
Leap into life, for Jesus comes.

Jesus, the God of might and love,
New moulds our limbs of cumbrous clay;
Quick as seraphic flames we move,
Active and young, and fair as they.

Our airy feet with unknown flight,
Swift as the motions of desire,
Run up the hills of heavenly light,
And leave the weltering world in fire.

The Day Dawning.

I. WATTS.

How long shall Death the tyrant reign
And triumph o'er the just,
While the rich blood of martyrs slain
Lies mingled with the dust?

When shall the tedious night be gone?
When will our Lord appear?
Our fond desires would pray him down,
Our love embrace him here.

Let faith arise and climb the hills,
And from afar descry
How distant are his chariot wheels,
And tell how fast they fly.

Lo, I behold the scattering shades;
The dawn of heaven appears;
The sweet immortal morning spreads
Its blushes round the spheres.

I see the Lord of glory come,
  And flaming guards around;
The skies divide to make him room,
  The trumpet shakes the ground.

I hear the voice, "Ye dead, arise!"
  And, lo! the graves obey,
And waking saints with joyful eyes
  Salute th' expectant day.

They leave the dust, and on the wing
  Rise to the middle air,
In shining garments meet their King,
  And low adore him there.

Oh may my humble spirit stand
  Amongst them clothed in white!
The meanest place at his right hand
  Is infinite delight.

How will our joy and wonder rise,
  When our returning King
Shall bear us homeward through the skies
  On love's triumphant wing!

The Bridegroom Cometh.

FROM THE GERMAN OF LAURENTIUS LAURENTII.

Rejoice, all ye believers,
And let your lights appear;
The evening is advancing,
And darker night is near;
The Bridegroom is arising,
And soon he draweth nigh;
Up! pray, and watch, and wrestle,—
At midnight comes the cry.

See that your lamps are burning;
Replenish them with oil,
And wait for your salvation,
The end of earthly toil;
The watchers on the mountain
Proclaim the Bridegroom near;
Go, meet him as he cometh,
With hallelujahs clear!

Ye wise and holy virgins,
Now raise your voices higher,
Till in songs of jubilee
They meet the angel-choir;
The marriage-feast is waiting,
The gates wide open stand;
Up! up! ye heirs of glory,
The Bridegroom is at hand!

Ye saints, who here in patience
  Your cross and sufferings bore,
Shall live and reign forever
  When sorrow is no more;
Around the throne of glory
  The Lamb ye shall behold,
In triumph cast before Him
  Your diadems of gold.

Palms of victory are there;
  There radiant garments are;
There stands the peaceful harvest,
  Beyond the reach of war;
There, after stormy winter,
  The flowers of earth arise,
And from the grave's long slumber
  Shall meet again our eyes.

Our Hope and Expectation,
  O Jesus, now appear!
Arise, thou Sun, so longed for,
  O'er this benighted sphere!
With hearts and hands uplifted,
  We plead, O Lord, to see
The day of earth's redemption
  That brings us unto thee!

Now the Pearly Gates Unfold.

FROM THE GERMAN OF W. C. DESSLER, BY MISS WINKWORTH.

Now the pearly gates unfold;
  Oh, thou Joy of highest heaven,
Who, ere earth was made, of old
  Light of light for light was given!
Hasten, Lord, and quickly come;
  Bring the bride thou hast betrothed,
  In thine own pure radiance clothed,
Safe to thine eternal home,
  Where no more the night of sin
  Spreads its fear and gloom within.

All my spirit thirsts to see,
  Lord, thy face unveiled and bright,
And to stand from sin set free,
  Spotless Lamb, amid thy light;
But I leave it, — thou dost well,
  And my heaven is here and now,
  Daystar of my soul, if thou
Wilt but deign in me to dwell;
  For without thee could there be
  Joy in heaven itself for me?

Bliss from thee my soul hath won,
  Spite of darkly threatening ill;
And my heart calls thee its Sun,
  And the sea of care grows still

In the shining of thy smile;
  And thy love's all-quickening ray
  Chases night and pain away,
That my heart grows light the while;
  Heavenly joys in thee are mine;
  Far from thee I mourn and pine.

Graft me into thee forever,
  Tree of Life, that I may grow
Stronger heavenward, drooping never
  For the sharpest storms that blow,
Bearing fruits of faith and truth;
  Then transplant me out of time
  Into that eternal clime
Where I shall renew my youth,
  When earth's withered leaves shall bloom
  Fresh in beauty from the tomb.

Life, to whom as to my Head
  I unite me, through my soul
Now thy quickening life-stream shed,
  And thy love's warm current roll,
Freshening all with strength and grace;
  Be thou mine, — I am thine own,
  Here and ever, thine alone;
All my hope in thee I place;
  Heaven and earth are nought to me,
  Safe, O Life of life, with thee!

VIII.

How Soon in Heaven?

How Long?

H. BONAR.

MY God, it is not fretfulness
That makes me say "How long?"
It is not heaviness of heart
That hinders me in song;
'Tis not despair of truth and right,
Nor coward dread of wrong.

But how can I, with such a hope
Of glory and of home,
With such a joy before my eyes,
Not wish the time were come,
Of years the jubilee, of days
The Sabbath and the sun?

These years, what ages they have been!
This life, how long it seems!
And how can I, in evil days,
'Mid unknown hills and streams,
But sigh for those of home and heart,
And visit them in dreams?

Yet peace, my heart, and hush, my tongue;
Be calm, my troubled breast;
Each restless hour is hastening on
The everlasting rest;
Thou knowest that the time thy God
Appoints for thee is best.

Let faith, not fear nor fretfulness,
Awake the cry, "How long?"
Let no faint-heartedness of soul
Damp thy aspiring song:
Right comes, truth dawns, the night departs
Of error and of wrong.

When comes His Hour?

FROM THE GERMAN OF K. J. P. SPITTA.

"JESUS' hour is not yet come;"
Let this word thy answer be,
Pilgrim, asking for thy home,
Longing to be blest and free
Yet a season tarry on,—
Nobly borne is nobly done.

While oppressing cares and fears
  Night and day no respite leave,
Still prolonged through many years,
  None to help thee or relieve;
Hold the word of promise fast,
Till deliverance comes at last.

Every creature-hope and trust,
  Every earthly prop or stay,
May lie prostrate in the dust,
  May have failed or passed away;
Then, when darkest falls the night,
Jesus comes, and all is light.

Yes, the Comforter draws nigh
  To the breaking, bursting heart,
For, with tender sympathy,
  He has seen and felt its smart;
Through its darkest hours of ill
He is waiting, watching still.

Dost thou ask when comes his hour?
  Then when it shall aid thee best;
Trust his faithfulness and power,
  Trust in him, and quiet rest;
Suffer on, and hope, and wait, —
Jesus never comes too late.

Blessed day, which hastens fast,
  End of conflict and of sin!
Death itself shall die at last,
  Heaven's eternal joys begin;
Then eternity shall prove
God is Light and God is Love.

A Little While.

GREVILLE.

A LITTLE while, and every fear
  That o'er the perfect day
Flings shadows dark and drear,
  Shall pass like mist away;
The secret tear, the anxious sigh,
  Shall pass into a smile;
Time changes to eternity,—
  We only wait a little while.

A little while, and every charm
  That steals away the heart,
And earthly joys that warm
  And lure us from our part,
Shall cease our heavenly views to dim;
  The world shall not beguile
Our ever-faithful thoughts from Him
  Who bade us wait a little while.

A little while, and all around,
  The earth, and sea, and sky,
The sunny light and sound
  Of nature's minstrelsy,
Shall be as they had never been,
  And we, so weak and vile,
Be creatures of a brighter scene,—
  We only wait a little while.

A Little Longer.

ADELAIDE A. PROCTOR.

A LITTLE longer still,—patience, beloved!—
  A little longer still, ere Heaven unroll
The glory, and the brightness, and the wonder,
  Eternal and divine, that waits thy soul.

A little longer ere life true, immortal,—
  Not this our shadowy life,—will be thine own,
And thou shalt stand where winged archangels worship,
  And trembling bow before the great white throne.

A little longer still, and heaven awaits thee,
  And fills thy spirit with a great delight;
Then our pale joys will seem a dream forgotten,
  Our sun a darkness, and our day a night.

A little longer, and thy heart, beloved,
  Shall beat forever with a love divine;
And joy so pure, so mighty, so eternal,
  No creature knows and lives, will then be thine.

A little longer yet, and angel voices
  Shall ring in heavenly chant upon thine ear;
Angels and saints await thee, and God needs thee;
  Beloved, can we bid thee linger here?

When Thou Wilt.

BAXTER.

Now it belongs not to my care
  Whether I die or live;
To love and serve thee is my share,
  And this thy grace must give.
If life be long, I will be glad,
  That I may long obey;
If short, yet why should I be sad,
  That shall have the same pay?

If death shall bruise this springing seed
  Before it comes to fruit,
The will with thee goes for the deed;
  Thy life was in the root.

Long life is a long grief and toil,
  And multiplieth faults;
In long wars he may have the foil
  That 'scapes in short assaults.

Christ leads us through no darker rooms
  Than he went through before;
He that into God's kingdom comes
  Must enter by this door.
Come, Lord, when grace hath made me meet
  Thy blessed face to see,
For if thy work on earth be sweet,
  What will thy glory be?

Then I shall end my sad complaints,
  And weary, sinful days,
And join with the triumphant saints
  That sing Jehovah's praise.
My knowledge of that life is small;
  The eye of faith is dim;
But 'tis enough that Christ knows all,
  And I shall be with him.

Daily Nearer.

EXAMINER.

NEARER home, nearer home!
However dark and lonely
The path through which we roam,
This is a journey only;
And though we oft, affrighted,
Shrink back with sigh and moan,
Our camp-fires still are lighted
"A day's march nearer home."

Nearer home, nearer home!
Oh, joy beyond expressing,
That over thorn and stone
Our feet are homeward pressing!
For though we leave behind us
Some buds of hope unblown,
The sunset still doth find us
"A day's march nearer home."

Nearer home, nearer home!
O many-mansioned dwelling,
Beneath thy shining dome
No tides of grief are swelling;
And toward thy fadeless glory
With eager haste we come,
Repeating earth's brief story,
"A day's march nearer home."

Nearer home, nearer home!
  Soon through its open portals
The ransomed hosts will come
  To welcome us immortals.
Then be the path before us
  With wrecks or roses strewn,
Each night we'll sing in chorus,
  "A day's march nearer home."

Nearer than when we Believed.

Knell of departed years,
  Thy voice is sweet to me;
It wakes no sad, foreboding fears,
Calls forth no sympathetic tears,
  Time's restless course to see;
    From hallowed ground
    I hear the sound,
Diffusing through the air a holy calm around.

Thou art the voice of love,
  To chide each doubt away;
And as thy murmur faintly dies,
Visions of past enjoyment rise
  In long and bright array;
    I hail the sign
    That love divine
Will o'er my future path in cloudless mercy shine.

Thou art the voice of hope;
The music of the spheres,
A song of blessings yet to come,
A herald from my future home,
My soul delighted hears:
By sin deceived,
By nature grieved,
Still am I nearer rest than when I first believed.

Thou art the voice of life,
A sound which seems to say,
Oh, prisoner in this gloomy vale,
Thy flesh shall faint, thy heart shall fail,
Yet fairer scenes thy spirit hail
That cannot pass away;
Here grief and pain
Thy steps detain;
There, in the image of the Lord, shalt thou with Jesus reign.

A few more Days.

H. BONAR.

A FEW more years shall roll,
A few more seasons come,
And we shall be with those that rest
Asleep within the tomb.

Then, O my Lord, prepare
  My soul for that great day;
Oh wash me in thy precious blood,
  And take my sins away!

A few more suns shall set
  O'er these dark hills of time,
And we shall be where suns are not,
  A far serener clime.
Then, O my Lord, prepare
  My soul for that blest day;
Oh wash me in thy precious blood,
  And take my sins away!

A few more storms shall beat
  On this wild, rocky shore,
And we shall be where tempests cease,
  And surges swell no more.
Then, O my Lord, prepare
  My soul for that calm day;
Oh wash me in thy precious blood,
  And take my sins away.

A few more struggles here,
  A few more partings o'er,
A few more toils, a few more tears,
  And we shall weep no more.

Then, O my Lord, prepare
  My soul for that blest day;
Oh wash me in thy precious blood,
  And take my sins away.

A few more Sabbaths here
  Shall cheer us on our way,
And we shall reach the endless rest,
  The eternal Sabbath-day.
Then, O my Lord, prepare
  My soul for that sweet day;
Oh wash me in thy precious blood,
  And take my sins away.

'Tis but a little while,
  And He shall come again
Who died that we might live, who lives
  That we with him may reign.
Then, O my Lord, prepare
  My soul for that glad day;
Oh wash me in thy precious blood,
  And take my sins away.

Soon Home.

H. BONAR.

BEYOND the smiling and the weeping
I shall be soon;
Beyond the waking and the sleeping,
Beyond the sowing and the reaping,
I shall be soon;
Love, rest, and home!
Sweet home!
Lord, tarry not, but come.

Beyond the blooming and the fading
I shall be soon;
Beyond the shining and the shading,
Beyond the hoping and the dreading,
I shall be soon.
Love, rest, and home!
Sweet home!
Lord, tarry not, but come.

Beyond the rising and the setting
I shall be soon;
Beyond the calming and the fretting,
Beyond remembering and forgetting,
I shall be soon.
Love, rest, and home!
Sweet home!
Lord, tarry not, but come.

Beyond the parting and the meeting
I shall be soon;
Beyond the farewell and the greeting,
Beyond the pulse's fever beating,
I shall be soon.
Love, rest, and home!
Sweet home!
Lord, tarry not, but come.

Beyond the frost-chain and the fever
I shall be soon;
Beyond the rock-waste and the river,
Beyond the ever and the never,
I shall be soon.
Love, rest, and home!
Sweet home!
Lord, tarry not, but come.

IX.

How Long in Heaven?

HOW LONG IN HEAVEN?

I. TILL THE RESURRECTION.

Burial and Resurrection.

GEORGE CROLY.

EARTH to earth, and dust to dust!
Here the evil and the just,
Here the youthful and the old,
Here the fearful and the bold,
Here the matron and the maid,
In one silent bed are laid;
Here the vassal and the king
Side by side lie withering;
Here the sword and sceptre rust:
"Earth to earth and dust to dust!"

Age on age shall roll along
O'er this pale and mighty throng;
Those that wept them, those that weep,
All shall with these sleepers sleep;

Brothers, sisters of the worm,
Summer's sun, or winter's storm
Song of peace, or battle's roar,
Ne'er shall break their slumbers more;
Death shall keep his silent trust:
"Earth to earth and dust to dust!"

But a day is coming fast,
Earth, thy mightiest and thy last;
It shall come in fear and wonder,
Heralded by trump and thunder;
It shall come in strife and toil;
It shall come in blood and spoil;
It shall come in empires' groans,
Burning temples, trampled thrones;
Then, ambition, rule thy lust:
"Earth to earth and dust to dust!"

Then shall come the judgment sign;
In the east the King shall shine,
Flashing from Heaven's golden gate,
Thousands, thousands round his state,
Spirits with the crown and plume.
Tremble, then, thou sullen tomb;
Heaven shall open on our sight,
Earth be turned to living light,
Kingdoms of the ransomed just:
"Earth to earth and dust to dust!"

Then thy mount, Jerusalem,
Shall be gorgeous as a gem;
Then shall in the desert rise
Fruits of more than Paradise;
Earth by angel feet be trod,
One great garden of her God,
Till are dried the martyrs' tears,
Through a thousand glorious years.
Now in hope of Him we trust:
"Earth to earth and dust to dust!"

Sleeping and Awaking.

FROM THE GERMAN OF P. F. HILLER.

The Shepherd, by his passion,
Made peace and wrought salvation;
To all in his good keeping
Now dying is but sleeping.

They go, not souls affrighted,
To judgment sternly cited;
They go from hardships dreary,
To rest like soldiers weary.

No fears the heart molesting,
From all life's trouble resting,
They wait the glad revival,
And sleep till its arrival.

They lay their toil-worn members
In death's cool, quiet chambers,
And, free from care and cumber,
Like children sink to slumber.

Safe in God's love that found them,
With Christ's strong arm around them,
And sealed by his good Spirit,
To die, why need they fear it?

Thy grace, O Lord, doth teach me
No harm through death can reach me
So let mine eyes, when closing,
Be on thy cross reposing;

This heart to thee be cleaving,
To its last beat believing;
Then, till the resurrection,
Give my poor dust protection.

Glad, then, be mine awaking,
My lips in praises breaking,
My body, clad with brightness,
Like the spring lily's whiteness!

Raised in Glory.

FROM THE LATIN OF PRUDENTIUS.

AH! hush now your mournful complainings,
  Nor, mothers, your sweet babes deplore;
This death we so shrink from but cometh
  The ruin of life to restore.

Who now would the sculptor's rich marble,
  Or beautiful sepulchres, crave?
We lay them but here in their slumber;
  This earth is a couch, not a grave.

For quickly the day is approaching
  When life through these cold limbs shall flow,
And the dwelling, restored to its inmate,
  With the old animation shall glow.

The body which lay in dishonor
  In the mouldering tomb to decay,
Rejoined to the spirit which dwelt there,
  Shall soar like a swift bird away.

The seed which we sow in its weakness
  In the spring shall rise green from the earth,
And the dead we thus mournfully bury
  In God's spring-time again shall shine forth.

Yet whilst, O our God, o'er the body
  Thou watchest, to mould it again,
What region of rest hast thou ordered
  Where the spirit unclothed may remain?

In the bosom of saints is her dwelling,
  Where the fathers and Lazarus are,
Whom the rich man, athirst, in his anguish
  Beholds in their bliss from afar.

We follow thy words, O Redeemer,
  When, trampling on Death in his pride,
Thou sentest to tread in thy footsteps
  The thief on the cross at thy side.

The bright way of Paradise opened,
  For every believer has space,
And that garden again we may enter
  Which the serpent once closed to our race.

Resurrection Hailed.

FROM THE GERMAN OF P. BUSCH, BY H. MILLS.

I HAIL the day, in prospect bright,
  When I from death awaking,
My Saviour God shall meet my sight,
  Forth in his glory breaking;

Then to the skies with joy I'll rise,
  Their crown of glory wearing
  Who love their Lord's appearing.

Thou, Lord, wilt in due time reveal
  That day of consummation,
When all thy saints from every ill
  Shall have complete salvation;
Then of thy love shall learn above,
  Through endless life, the measure,
  Of grace thy boundless treasure.

That life thou wilt to me impart;
  Thou art my hope unceasing;
Thy coming shall rejoice my heart,
  My prisoned dust releasing;
Nor need I fear before thy bar
  The scoffers to resemble,
  Who shall in anguish tremble;

While I, in wonder and delight,
  Shall stand, dear Lord, before thee,
With ransomed sinners on thy right,
  And then in heaven adore thee.
With hopes so high thy grace supply,
  To fit me for thy favor,
  And for thy joys forever!

The Glorious Coming.

T. LAURIE.

OUR Saviour shall descend again,
Earth's buried millions raising;
With him shall come a glorious train,
Adoring him and praising.
Raise high the song that loud and long
Before him ceaseth never,
Till, casting down each golden crown,
All worship him forever.

What though these bodies lie in dust
Before that glad appearing?
Yet shall they stand among the just,
Our Saviour's image wearing.
Raise high the song that loud and long
Before him ceaseth never,
Till, casting down each golden crown,
All worship him forever.

What though earth's gathering tempests lower,
And ages pass in sadness?
Their darkest hour shall swell the power
And glory of that gladness.
Raise high the song that loud and long
Before him ceaseth never,
Till, casting down each golden crown
All worship him forever.

Then safe at last the blessed throng,
  Set free from tribulation,
Forever praise, in holy song,
  The God of their salvation.
    Raise high the song that loud and long
      Before him ceaseth never,
    Till, casting down each golden crown,
      All worship him forever.

The Evening Watch.

HENRY VAUGHAN.

BODY.

Farewell! I goe to sleep; but when
The day-star springs, I'll wake again.

SOUL.

Goe, sleep in peace; and when thou lyest
Unnumbered in thy dust, when all this frame
Is but one dramme, and what thou now descriest
  In sev'rall parts shall want a name,
Then may His peace be with thee, and each dust
Writ in His book, who ne'er betrayed man's trust!

BODY.

Amen! but hark, ere we two stray,—
How many hours, dost think, 'till day?

SOUL.

Ah, go; thou'rt weak, and sleepie. Heaven
Is a plain watch, and without figures winds
All ages up; who drew this circle, even
He fills it; dayes and hours are blinds.
Yet this take with thee: the last gasp of time
Is thy first breath, and man's eternall prime.

Renaissance.

JAMES BEATTIE.

Yet such the destiny of all on earth;
So flourishes and fades majestic man;
Fair is the bud his vernal morn brings forth,
And fostering gales a while the nursling fan.
Oh smile, ye heavens serene; ye mildews wan,
Ye blighting whirlwinds, spare his balmy prime,
Nor lessen of his life the little span.
Borne on the swift though silent wings of time,
Old age comes on apace to ravage all the clime.

And be it so. Let those deplore their doom
Whose hope still grovels in this dark sojourn;
But lofty souls, who look beyond the tomb,
Can smile at fate, and wonder how they mourn.
Shall spring to these sad scenes no more return?

Is yonder wave the sun's eternal bed?
  Soon shall the orient with new lustre burn,
And spring shall soon her vital influence shed,
Again attune the grove, again adorn the mead.

Shall I be left abandoned in the dust,
  When fate, relenting, lets the flower revive?
Shall nature's voice, to man alone unjust,
  Bid him, though doomed to perish, hope to live?
  Is it for this fair virtue oft must strive
With disappointment, penury, and pain?
  No; heaven's immortal spring shall yet arrive,
And man's majestic beauty bloom again,
Bright through the eternal year of love's triumphant reign.

Reappearing.

H. BONAR.

THE star is not extinguished when it sets
  Upon the dull horizon; but it goes
To shine in other skies, then reappear
  In ours, as fresh as when it first arose.

The river is not lost when o'er the rock
  It pours its flood into the abyss below;
Its scattering force regathering from the shock,
  It hastens onward with yet fuller flow.

The bright sun dies not when the shadowing orb
 Of the eclipsing moon obscures its ray;
It still is shining on, and soon to us
 Will burst undimmed into the joy of day.

The lily dies not when both flower and leaf
 Fade, and are strewed upon the chill, sad ground;
Gone for shelter to its mother earth,
 'Twill rise, re-bloom, and shed its fragrance round.

The dew-drop dies not when it leaves the flower,
 And passes upward on the beam of morn;
It does but hide itself in light on high,
 To its loved flower at twilight to return.

The fine gold has not perished when the flame
 Seizes upon it with consuming glow;
In freshened splendor it comes forth anew,
 To sparkle on the monarch's throne or brow.

Thus nothing dies, or only dies to live,—
 Star, stream, sun, flower, the dew-drop, and the gold;
Each goodly thing, instinct with buoyant hope,
 Hastes to put on its purer, finer mould.

So, in the quiet joy of kindly trust,
 We bid each parting saint a brief farewell;
Weeping, yet smiling, we commit their dust
 To the safe keeping of the silent cell.

Softly within that peaceful resting-place
  We place their wearied limbs, and bid the clay
Press lightly on them, till the night be past,
  And the far east give note of coming day.

The day of reappearing, how it speeds!
  He who is true and faithful speaks the word;
Then shall we ever be with those we love;
  Then shall we be forever with the Lord.

The shout is heard; the archangel's voice goes forth;
  The trumpet sounds; the dead awake and sing;
The living put on glory; one glad band,
  They hasten up to meet their coming King!

Short death and darkness, endless life and light!
  Short dimming, endless shining in yon sphere,
Where all is incorruptible and pure,
  The joy without the pain, the smile without the
      tear.

The Day Breaketh.

FROM THE GERMAN OF C. C. STURM.

HARK! the trump of God is sounding,
The archangel's shout the call resounding,
  Arise, ye saints, and leave the tomb;
Children of your heavenly Father,

To him from your dispersions gather;
The Lord of glory calls you home;
Behold the morning break;
Death's night is gone; awake!
Hallelujah!
Now is prepared
Your full reward;
That day, the last great day, is here!

Earth, and sea, and hell, are quaking;
Now the redeemed to life are waking;
To new and perfect life they rise;
Jesus comes in glory's brightness,
Before him mercy, truth, uprightness, —
How fair their crown! how rich the prize!
They live with God's dear Son,
Their light his shining throne;
Shout hosannas;
Redeemer, thou
Dost give us now
Sure mansions of eternal peace.

Praise shall be our glad employment
Through endless day of pure enjoyment;
What stores in thee of grace unknown!
Joys are now all hope excelling;
New wonders still thou art revealing,
Our Friend, and God's beloved Son.

Never to eye appeared,
Such things were never heard,—
Thine the glory;
Eternally,
O Lord, to thee
New songs and honors be addressed!

Awake, Awake!

FROM THE GERMAN OF PHILIP NICOLAI.

Awake, awake, for night is flying,
The watchmen on the heights are crying;
Awake, Jerusalem, at last!
Midnight hears the welcome voices,
And at the thrilling cry rejoices:
Come forth, ye virgins, night is past;
The Bridegroom comes; awake;
Your lamps with gladness take;
Hallelujah!
And for his marriage-feast prepare,
For ye must go to meet him there.

Zion hears the watchmen singing,
And all her heart with joy is springing;
She wakes; she rises from her gloom;
For her Lord comes down all-glorious,
The strong in grace, in truth victorious;

Her star is risen, her Light is come.
Ah, come, thou blessed Lord,
O Jesus, Son of God,
Hallelujah!
We follow till the halls we see
Where thou hast bid us sup with thee.

Now let all the heavens adore thee,
And men and angels sing before thee,
With harp and cymbal's clearest tone;
Of one pearl each shining portal,
Where we are with the choir immortal
Of angels round thy dazzling throne;
Nor eye hath seen, nor ear
Hath yet attained to hear
What there is ours;
But we rejoice, and sing to thee
Our hymn of joy eternally.

Ascend, Beloved.

H. BONAR.

ASCEND, beloved, to the joy;
The festal day has come;
To-night the Lamb doth feast his own,
To-night he with his bride sits down,
To-night puts on the spousal crown,
In the great upper room.

Ascend, beloved, to the love;
  This is the day of days;
To-night the bridal song is sung,
To-night ten thousand harps are strung,
In sympathy with heart and tongue,
  Unto the Lamb's high praise.

The festal lamps are lighting now
  In the great marriage-hall;
By angel-hands the board is spread;
By angel-hands the sacred bread
Is on the golden table laid;
  The King his own doth call.

The gems are gleaming from the roof,
  Like stars in night's round dome;
The festal wreaths are hanging there,
The festal fragrance fills the air,
And flowers of heaven, divinely fair,
  Unfold their happy bloom.

Long, long deferred, now come at last,
  The Lamb's glad wedding-day;
The guests are gathering to the feast,
The seats in heavenly order placed,
The royal throne above the rest;
  How bright the new array!

Sorrow and sighing are no more;
  The weeping hours are past;
To-night the waiting will be done,
To-night the wedding-robe put on,
The glory and the joy begun;
  The crown has come at last.

Without, within, is light, is light;
  Around, above, is love, is love;
We enter, to go out no more;
We raise the song unsung before;
We doff the sackcloth that we wore;
  For all is joy above.

Ascend, beloved, to the life;
  Our days of death are o'er;
Mortality has done its worst;
The fetters of the tomb are burst;
The last has now become the first,
  Forever, evermore.

Ascend, beloved, to the feast;
  Make haste, thy day is come;
Thrice blest are they the Lamb doth call
To share the heavenly festival
In the new Salem's palace-hall,
  Our everlasting home.

II. FOR EVER AND EVER.

Life Eternal.

BRIEF life is here our portion,
Brief sorrow, short-lived care;
The life that knows no ending,
The tearless life, is there.
Reward of grace how wondrous!
Short toil, eternal rest!
Oh, miracle of mercy,
That rebels should be blest!

That we, with sin polluted,
Should have our home so high!
That we should dwell in mansions
Beyond the starry sky!
And now we fight the battle,
And then we wear the crown
Of full and everlasting
And ever-bright renown.

I know not, oh! I know not
What social joys are there;
What pure, unfading glory;
What light beyond compare;

And when I fain would sing them,
  My spirit fails and faints,
And vainly strives to image
  The assembly of the saints.

There is the throne of David,
  And there, from toil released,
The shout of them that triumph,
  The song of them that feast;
O garden free from sorrow!
  O plains that fear no strife!
O princely bowers all-blooming!
  O realm and home of life!

For Evermore.

DUBLIN UNIVERSITY MAGAZINE.

Two worlds there are. To one our eyes we strain,
Whose magic joys we shall not see again;
Bright haze of morning veils its glimmering shore;
    Ah! truly breathed we there
    Intoxicating air;
Glad were our hearts in that sweet realm of nevermore.

The lover there drank her delicious breath
Whose love has yielded since to change or death;
The mother kissed her child whose days are o'er.
Alas! too soon have fled
The irreclaimable dead;
We see them — visions strange — amid the nevermore.

The merry song some maidens used to sing,
The brown, brown hair, that once was wont to cling
To temples long clay cold — to the very core
They strike our weary hearts,
As some vexed memory starts
From that long-faded land, the realm of nevermore.

It is perpetual summer there. But here
Sadly we remember rivers clear,
And harebells quivering on the meadow floor;
For brighter bells and bluer,
For tender hearts and truer,
People that happy land, the realm of nevermore.

Upon the frontier of this shadowy land
We, pilgrims of eternal sorrow, stand;
What realm lies forward, with its happier store
Of forests green and deep,
Of valleys hushed in sleep,
And lakes most peaceful? 'Tis the land of evermore.

Very far off its marble cities seem;
Very far off, beyond our sensual dream,
Its woods unruffled by the wild wind's roar;
Yet does the turbulent surge
Howl on its very verge;
One moment, and we breathe within the evermore.

They whom we loved and lost so long ago
Dwell in those cities, far from mortal woe,
Haunt those fresh woodlands, whence sweet carollings soar.
Eternal peace have they;
God wipes their tears away;
They drink that river of life which flows for evermore.

Thither we hasten through these regions dim;
But, lo! the wide wings of the seraphim
Shine in the sunset! on that joyous shore
Our lightened hearts shall know
The life of long ago;
The sorrow-burdened past shall fade for evermore.

Soon and Forever.

J. S. MONSELL.

"SOON and forever!"
  Such promise our trust,
Though ashes to ashes,
  And dust unto dust, —
Soon and forever
  Our union shall be
Made perfect, our glorious
  Redeemer, in thee.
When the sins and the sorrows
  Of time shall be o'er,
Its pangs and its partings
  Remembered no more,
When life cannot fail,
  And when death cannot sever
Christians with Christ shall be
  Soon and forever.

Soon and forever
  The breaking of day
Shall drive all the night-clouds
  Of sorrow away.
Soon and forever
  We'll see as we're seen,
And learn the deep meaning
  Of things that have been;

When fightings without us,
  And fears from within,
Shall weary no more
  In the warfare of sin;
Where tears, and where fears,
  And where death shall be never,
Christians with Christ shall be
  Soon and forever.

Soon and forever
  The work shall be done,
The warfare accomplished,
  The victory won;
Soon and forever
  The soldier lay down
His sword for a harp,
  And his cross for a crown.
Then droop not in sorrow,
  Despond not in fear;
A glorious to-morrow
  Is brightening and near,
When, blessed reward
  Of each faithful endeavor,
Christians with Christ shall be
  Soon and forever.

Ever with the Lord.

J. MONTGOMERY.

"FOREVER with the Lord!"
  Amen; so let it be;
Life from the dead is in that word,
  'Tis immortality.

Here in the body pent,
  Absent from him I roam,
Yet nightly pitch my moving tent
  A day's march nearer home.

My Father's house on high,
  Home of my soul, how near,
At times, to faith's foreseeing eye
  Thy golden gates appear!

Ah! then my spirit faints
  To reach the land I love,
The bright inheritance of saints,
  Jerusalem above.

Yet clouds will intervene,
  And all my prospect flies;
Like Noah's dove, I flit between
  Rough seas and stormy skies.

Anon the clouds depart,
  The winds and waters cease,
While sweetly o'er my gladdened heart
  Expands the bow of peace.

Beneath its glowing arch,
  Along the hallowed ground,
I see cherubic armies march,
  A camp of fire around.

I hear at morn and even,
  At noon and midnight hour,
The choral harmonies of heaven
  Earth's Babel-tongues o'erpower.

Then, then I feel that He
  (Remembered or forgot),
The Lord, is never far from me,
  Though I perceive him not.

In darkness as in light,
  Hidden alike from view,
I sleep, I wake, as in His sight
  Who looks all nature through.

All that I am, have been,
  All that I yet may be,
He sees at once, as he hath seen,
  And shall forever see.

How can I meet his eyes?
  Mine on the cross I cast,
And own my life a Saviour's prize,
  Mercy from first to last.

"Forever with the Lord!"
  Father, if 'tis thy will,
The promise of that faithful word
  Even here to me fulfil!

Be thou at my right hand,
  Then can I never fail;
Uphold thou me, and I shall stand;
  Fight, and I must prevail:

So when my latest breath
  Shall rend the veil in twain,
By death I shall escape from death,
  And life eternal gain.

Knowing as I am known,
  How shall I love that word,
And oft repeat before the throne,
  "Forever with the Lord!"

Then, though the soul enjoy
  Communion high and sweet,
While worms this body must destroy,
  Both shall in glory meet.

The trump of final doom
  Will speak the self-same word,
And heaven's voice thunder through the tomb,
  "Forever with the Lord!"

The tomb shall echo deep
  That death-awakening sound;
The saints shall hear it in their sleep,
  And answer from the ground.

Then upward as they fly,
  That resurrection-word
Shall be their shout of victory,
  "Forever with the Lord!"

That resurrection-word,
  That shout of victory,
Once more, "Forever with the Lord!"
  Amen; so let it be.

THE END.

www.ingramcontent.com/pod-product-compliance
Lightning Source LLC
Chambersburg PA
CBHW030903270326
41929CB00008B/555

* 9 7 8 3 3 3 7 0 8 3 0 1 4 *